E. NOELTNER

Behind the Scenes:
Practical Entertainment Law

Michael I. Rudell

Law & Business, Inc./Harcourt Brace Jovanovich, Publishers

Requests for permission to make copies of any part
of the work should be mailed to:
Permissions, Law & Business, Inc.
757 Third Avenue, New York, N.Y. 10017

Printed in the United States of America

Library of Congress Cataloging in Publication Data:

Rudell, Michael I.
  Behind the scenes: practical entertainment law.

  Includes index.
  1. Performing arts—Law and legislation—United States.
2. Entertainers—Legal status, laws, etc.—
United States. 3. Artists' contracts—United States.
I. Title
KF4290.R82   1983   344.73'097   83-22201
ISBN 0-15-004363-5   347.30497

To Alice and Liza

ACKNOWLEDGEMENTS

To the remarkable attorneys of Franklin, Weinrib, Rudell & Vassallo, P.C., and particularly Rose Schwartz, Kenneth Kaufman and Neil Rosini for their assistance in the preparation of several articles.

To the New York Law Journal for affording the subject of Entertainment Law a position of prominence in a respected publication.

To Stephen Glasser for supporting and implementing the publication of the first Entertainment Law columns.

To Len Franklin and John Vassallo.

To Joyce Benjamin for years of tolerance and Paulette Strauss and Bruce Townsend for their invaluable assistance.

To Anna and Joseph L. Rudell, with thanks too infrequently expressed.

Michael I. Rudell, 1983

CONTENTS

INTRODUCTION

A well-known case decided by the U.S. Supreme Court involved the claim that a news broadcast of the entire fifteen second act of a human cannonball violated his right of publicity. The facts and decision in this case illustrate why practicing and writing on the subject of entertainment law is a rewarding experience: the legal issues often are intricate; knowledge of the business practices is integral to an understanding of the subject; the parties to disputes often are public figures, and the fact situations tend to keep one interested.

Not all of the articles contained in this book concern judicial decisions. Several review statutes or present analyses of elements to be considered in drafting agreements or developing productions. Others explore trends in the industry and technological developments. Although all have been selected with the hope that, individually and collectively, they provide useful information regarding the business and legal aspects of the entertainment industry, this book is not intended to serve as a treatise on the subject of entertainment law.

All of the selections originally were published in the *New York Law Journal*, with the exception of those indicated as having been prepared for *Variety* or as the subject of a speech. Some have been revised from the original version. Each is intended to stand on its own and, although much thought has been given to the classification and placement of the pieces, it is not necessary that they be read in sequence.

Michael I. Rudell, 1983

Chapter One

Privacy, Publicity and Defamation

A Public Figure's Right of Privacy: The *Ann-Margret* Decision

Actress Ann-Margret's semi-clothed appearance in a single scene of the motion picture "Magic" generated unanticipated and unwanted publicity for her in the form of a series of revealing photographs in the magazine, *High Society Celebrity Skin*. Claiming violation of her rights of privacy and publicity she sought injunctive relief and damages in the U.S. District Court for the Southern District in New York under Section 51 of the New York Civil Rights Law.[1]

Although evidencing sympathy for Ann-Margret's predicament of receiving publicity in what it described as a "tacky" magazine, the Court nevertheless granted defendants' motion for summary judgment.

Ann-Margret's election to appear partially disrobed in "Magic" was based, she stated, on "artistic" reasons and "script necessities." The performance constituted only the second semi-nude screen appearance of her career and the actress took the precaution of requiring that the minimum number of necessary personnel be present during the filming, and that no still photographs of the scene be taken. Despite these precautions, defendants' first edition of *Celebrity Skin*, entitled "Special Collector's Edition No. 1," featured a five page primarily photographic article on Ann-Margret, including a picture taken from "Magic" in which according to the Court "one of her breasts is quite visible."

Ann-Margret's first claim against *High Society* alleged a violation of her right of privacy based on Section 51 of the New York Civil Rights Law. This section, which allows for injunctive relief or damages to any person whose name, portrait or picture is used within New York for advertising purposes or for the purposes of trade without written consent, if read literally "would provide an extremely broad course of action applicable to virtually all uses of a person's name or picture, including use by the news media."[2] Thus,

this provision has been narrowly construed by courts, especially in
the realm of "public figures," to avoid the potential conflict between
the right of privacy and the guarantee in the First Amendment of
protection for "the free dissemination of thoughts, ideas, newsworthy events, and matters of public interest."[3] As has been noted by
New York courts, "freedom of speech and the press under the First
Amendment transcends the right to privacy."[4]

A public figure, by virtue of his or her status as such, does not
lose all rights of privacy. For example, courts have protected Jac-
queline Onassis and her family from unwarranted intrusions,[5] and
Muhammad Ali, when an unauthorized nude drawing of him accompanied by a "plainly fictional and allegedly libelous bit of dog-
gerel" appeared in a magazine.[6] But once a person has sought publicity, his rights can be severely circumscribed by virtue of his
newsworthiness and he cannot at his whim withdraw the events of
his life from public scrutiny. As a result, the use of a public figure's
name or picture in the context of an event within the orbit of public
interest can rarely be the basis for an actionable claim under Section
51.

In the present case, Ann-Margret chose to appear partially nude
in one scene of a film which she knew would be widely distributed.
Having consented to be viewed in a certain manner during the course
of a public performance, she could not successfully argue that a
subsequent faithful reproduction of that appearance constituted an
invasion of privacy.

Further, although the Court may have sympathized with her
feelings, neither the fact that Ann-Margret did not like the manner
in which she was portrayed, nor the medium in which her picture
was reproduced, nor her belief that the reproduction caused her
embarrassment, could expand her rights or create a cause of action
under Section 51. When there has been a public performance, especially by a public figure, reproduction of that performance in the
manner here involved does not give rise to such a cause of action
under Section 51.

In a footnote to the decision the Court distinguished the *Ann-
Margret* situation from a case brought by Barbara Streisand against
High Society.[7] There, a preliminary injunction was issued (without
opinion) to prevent the magazine from publishing "outtakes" (deleted material) from the film "The Owl and the Pussycat." Although

Streisand, like Ann-Margret evidently consented to the photography which occurred, the *Streisand* case (to the extent it may have precedental value) differed from the *Ann-Margret* case in that the outtakes never were shown to the public. Also, in the *Streisand* case one of the plaintiffs was a copyright owner of the film, a fact not present in the instant case.

The discussion by the court of plaintiff's claim based upon an invasion of her right of publicity was relatively brief. That right, which has been viewed as both a privacy right and a property right, is based on the right of an individual to exploit the publicity value of his name or likeness for pecuniary value and includes, by way of example, the right of a celebrity to grant the exclusive privilege of publishing his photograph in connection with a product or to authorize the use of his likeness in an advertisement.[8] Here the Court found that the use of the photographs in question by a magazine specializing in the printing of photographs of "well-known women caught in the most revealing situations and positions," although understandably distasteful to the actress, did not constitute a use for trade or advertising purposes. Relying on *Paulsen v. Personality Posters, Inc.*[9] the opinion stated that "to the extent a right of publicity exists at all under New York law, it does not invest a prominent person with the right to exploit financially every public use of name or picture." Further, it is well established that a simple use in a magazine published and sold for profit does not constitute a use for trade or advertising sufficient to make out an actionable claim.

It will be of interest to note whether the fact that a performer may have no legal recourse against the publication of a pictorial review in a magazine such as *High Society Celebrity Skin* dissuades that performer in the future from appearing in scenes calling for brief nudity or other unusual poses, regardless of the artistic merit involved.

FOOTNOTES

1. Ann-Margret v. High Society Magazine, Inc., 498 F. Supp. 401 (S.D.N.Y. 1980).
2. *Id.*
3. Time, Inc. v. Hill, 385 U.S. 374, 382 (1967).

4.   Namath v. Sports Illustrated, 80 Misc.2d 531, 535, 363 N.Y.S.2d 276, 280 (N.Y. Co. 1975), aff'd, 48 A.D. 2d 487, 371 N.Y.S.2d 10 (1st Dep't 1975), aff'd, 39 N.Y.2d 397, 352 N.E.2d 587 (1976).

5.   Galella v. Onassis, 487 F.2d 986 (2d Cir. 1973).

6.   Ali v. Playgirl, 447 F. Supp. 723 (S.D.N.Y. 1978).

7.   Streisand v. High Society Magazine, Inc., No 79-5132 (S.D.N.Y., filed September 26, 1979).

8.   Haelan v. Topps Chewing Gum, 202 F.2d 866 (2d Cir. 1953), cert. denied, 346 U.S. 816 (1953).

9.   59 Misc. 2d 444, 450, 299 N.Y.S.2d 501, 508 (Sup. Ct. N.Y. Co. 1968).

Right of Publicity Subsumed in New York Privacy Statute

The law in the right of privacy area remains "that of a haystack in a hurricane"[1] following a decision of the New York Appellate Division regarding the well-known model Christie Brinkley.[2]

The defendants in the action were Elite Model Management Corp. ("Elite"), Brinkley's former model agency, its president John Casablancas ("Casablancas"); Galaxy Publishing Corp. ("Galaxy"), the publisher and distributor of the poster on which Brinkley's likeness appeared; and two retail stores.

In 1979, Casablancas, in his personal capacity, entered into a licensing agreement with Galaxy to produce a series of posters bearing the photographs of several top models, including Brinkley. Galaxy's right to print, publish and vend the posters was conditioned upon Casablancas' obtaining the consent of the models.

Brinkley, having agreed to participate in the project, chose her hair stylist, makeup artist and bathing suit and posed in a photographic session. While she was being photographed, a cable television production company filmed the session for use in what eventually became a television program entitled "Beautiful, Baby, Beautiful" which was transmitted throughout the United States on three occasions by Home Box Office. Brinkley appeared in that cablecast in the same pose and bathing suit as she appeared in the subject poster. Further, a photograph of Brinkley, almost identical to the poster photograph, appeared with her consent in a print advertisement for the Home Box Office program.

During the two months following the photographic session, Brinkley reviewed color transparencies and poster proofs which Galaxy had developed. The photograph which eventually appeared in the subject poster was selected by Casablancas and Galaxy. After the photograph had been retouched at Brinkley's request, Galaxy printed and began commercial distribution of the poster in March, 1980. Two retail stores purchased copies of the poster; both purchases were made without the knowledge or consent of Brinkley, Casablancas or Elite, although Galaxy contended that at some time prior to October 3, 1979 Casablancas had confirmed orally that he had obtained the consent of Brinkley to proceed with the project. Brinkley never signed a written release authorizing distribution of her photograph or likeness on the poster.

When Casablancas learned of the unauthorized sale of the poster, he terminated his contract with Galaxy. Thereafter, Brinkley, alleging unauthorized commercial exploitation of her name and picture by the production of the poster, with consequent injury to her feelings and wrongful invasion of her right of publicity, commenced an action seeking a preliminary injunction against further distribution of the poster, a permanent injunction and compensatory and exemplary damages under Section 51 of the Civil Rights Law. She also sought an accounting, based upon an alleged breach of fiduciary duty, of all profits received by Casablancas and Elite from the sale and distribution of the poster and compensatory and exemplary damages against Casablancas, Elite and Galaxy for conspiracy to defraud.

Holding that Section 51 of the Civil Rights Law never was intended to afford a cause of action for invasion of privacy to one who, with legitimate expectations of sharing in profits, willingly and knowingly participated in a project which would publicize her name and picture, Special Term granted defendants partial summary judgment and dismissed the right of privacy claims. Only plaintiff appealed from that decision and, accordingly, the opinion of the Appellate Division concerned solely whether a triable issue of fact existed as to Brinkley's right of privacy causes of action.

The relevant portion of Section 51 is as follows:

"Any person whose name, portrait or picture is used within this state for advertising purposes or for the purpose of trade without the written consent first obtained as above provided may maintain an equitable action in the Supreme Court of this state against the person, firm or corporation so using his name, portrait or picture, to prevent and restrain the use thereof; and may also sue and recover damages for any injuries sustained by reason of such use and if the defendant shall have knowingly used such person's name, portrait or picture in such manner as is forbidden or declared to be unlawful by the last section, the jury, in its discretion, may award exemplary damages."[3]

The application of this Section has been restricted to avoid conflicts with the freedoms of speech and press guaranteed under the First Amendment. "Thus, the right of privacy of those who, voluntarily or otherwise, have become public figures and in whose activities a legitimate public interest exists, is significantly curtailed."[4] However, a public figure does retain the independent right to have his or her personality, even if newsworthy, free from commercial exploitation by another.

Acknowledging that the sale of the poster was a use of plaintiff's photograph for trade purposes, defendants claimed that, by performing in the television broadcast "Beautiful, Baby, Beautiful," plaintiff waived her right of publicity to any likeness and image extracted from that performance. In support of this position, defendants cited the decision in the *Ann-Margret* case.[5]

The Appellate Division distinguished the *Ann-Margret* case from the subject action by noting that Brinkley's photograph and the manner in which it was designed to be used did not involve a subject of general interest, and that, unlike the *Ann-Margret* case, the photograph which was published did not appear as part of the public performance in which Brinkley appeared.

The Court noted that defendants never claimed that Brinkley's written consent to a use of the photograph ever was given and stated that written consent is required under Sections 50 and 51; oral consent is not a defense, being relevant only on the question of damages.

Nor will previous written consent to the use of other photographs be deemed implied authorization. "That [plaintiff] may have voluntarily on occasion surrendered her privacy, for a price or gratuitously, does not forever forfeit for anyone's commercial profit so much of her privacy as she has not relinquished."[6]

The Court then dealt with the contention of the defendants that the actual complaint of the plaintiff was injury to her right of publicity, a cause of action which, proprietary in nature, was not pleaded by plaintiff and is not within the ambit of Civil Rights Law Section 51.

Although the United States Court of Appeals for the Second Circuit, in construing New York law, has found that the so-called right of publicity does, in fact, exist independent of the statutory right of privacy, New York courts never have explicitly recognized the non-statutory right of publicity.

A plaintiff asserting invasion of his right of privacy seeks to minimize the intrusion or publication of the damaging matter while the plaintiff asserting violation of his right of publicity does not necessarily object to the commercial exploitation so long as the exploitation is at his behest and he is receiving the profits. In *Zacchini v. Scripps-Howard Broadcasting Company*,[7] the U.S. Supreme Court stated that the State's interest in the protection of the right of publicity is closely analogous to the goals of the patent and copyright laws, focusing on the right of the individual to reap the reward of his endeavors and having little to do with protecting feelings and reputations.

Courts applying New York law have found the right of publicity to be a valid transferrable property right but have found the statutory right of privacy to be neither descendible nor assignable.

Although there has been no explicit recognition by New York courts of a separate and distinct common law right of publicity, the Appellate Division noted that some New York courts have suggested that such a right might exist.[8]

"[A]ny suggestion in these decisions of the existence of a right of publicity independent of the statutory right of privacy obviously arose because Sections 50 and 51 of the Civil Rights Law, due to their limited application, would not accommodate the privacy claim in the particular case."[9]

The Court then stated that irrespective of whether a separate and distinct common law right of publicity exists in this state, it believes that the so-called right of publicity is subsumed in Sections 50 and 51 of the Civil Rights Law to the extent that even a public figure has a privacy interest which finds recognition in the statute and for the violation of which a remedy of monetary redress is provided.

"The confusion over whether the statutory right of privacy embraces the public figure's commercial interest in the exploitation of his personality is undoubtedly due, in part, to the statute's historical origins and the popular and ready usage of the term 'privacy' in referring to the right which it encompasses. But the statute does not distinguish between the private person for whom injured feelings may be the paramount concern and the public figure whose right of privacy is limited in any event by public interest consideration, but whose economic interests are affected by the wrongful exploitation of his or her name or likeness. The wrong consists of only two elements; the commercial use of a person's name or photograph and the failure to procure the person's written consent for such use. The damages that flow from the confluence of these two events should be compensable whether the injury is to one's feelings or to his 'property' interest. Both injuries are caused by the same wrong and should be redressed by the same cause of action."[10]

Noting the argument of the defendants that the evidentiary facts offered by the plaintiff constituted a cause of action for violation of right of publicity rather than invasion of right of privacy, the Court concluded that a pleading will not be dismissed for insufficiency merely because it is inartistically drawn. "Thus, even if we were to accept defendants' contention that an injury to plaintiff's right of publicity, exclusively proprietary in nature, is not within the purview of Section 51 of the Civil Rights Law but reposes instead in the common law, we would not be justified in dismissing the statutory right of privacy claims since the complaint may be fairly and reasonably interpreted as pleading a right of publicity claim."[11]

Holding that the admitted failure of defendant Galaxy to have obtained Brinkley's written consent prior to the unauthorized sale of the poster was dispositive on the issue of liability under the Civil Rights Law, the Court granted Brinkley summary judgment on the first cause of action against Galaxy and the retail stores and granted her partial summary judgment on liability only on the second cause of action against Galaxy.

The Court upheld the grant of summary judgment to Elite and Casablancas and the dismissal of the right of privacy claims against them on the grounds that the authorized delivery of plaintiff's photographs for the limited purpose of producing a poster proof could not be construed as a "use" in violation of the Civil Rights Law merely because Galaxy subsequently, without consent and in violation of its agreement with Casablancas, sold the poster. Further, Galaxy had written to Casablancas requesting written confirmation that consent had been obtained from Brinkley to manufacture and distribute the posters and no such confirmation ever was forthcoming. Galaxy never pursued this request.[12] Also, Elite in no way contributed to or participated in the unauthorized publication of the poster.

The decision of the Appellate Division leaves open several questions which were raised in defendants' brief. If the right of publicity is subsumed in Sections 50 and 51 of the Civil Rights Law, to the extent that a public figure has a privacy interest which is recognizable in the statute and for the violation of which a remedy of monetary redress is provided, is that right of publicity assignable and descendible?

Will a cause of action for violation of a right of publicity under Section 51 be governed by the one year statute of limitations pertaining thereto or the six year statute of limitations pertaining to a misappropriation of property? Is the pleading of an economic loss a prerequisite to a successful right of publicity cause of action if that right is subsumed in the Civil Rights Law?

Further, it will be interesting to see how, on the basis of the Brinkley decision, a federal court interprets the law of New York in the next right of publicity case.

FOOTNOTES

1.   Ettore v. Philco Television Broadcasting Corp., 229 F.2d 481, 485, (3rd Cir. 1956), *cert. denied,* 351 U.S. 929 (1956).

2.   Brinkley v. Casablancas, 80 A.D.2d 428, 438 N.Y.S.2d 1004 (1981).

3.   N.Y. Civil Rights Law, Section 51.

4.   Koussevitsky v. Allen, Towne & Heathe, Inc., 188 Misc. 479, 68 N.Y.S.2d 779, (Sup. Ct. 1947), *aff'd,* 272 App. Div. 759, 69 N.Y.S.2d 432 (1947).

5.   Ann-Margret v. High Society Magazine, Inc., 498 F. Supp. 401 (S.D.N.Y. 1980).

6.   Booth v. Curtis Publishing Co., 15 A.D.2d 343, 223 N.Y.S.2d 737 (1st Dep't 1962), *aff'd,* 11 N.Y.2d 907, 182 N.E.2d 812 (1962).

7.   43 U.S. 562 (1977).

8.   Frosch v. Grosset & Dunlap, Inc., 75 A.D.2d 768, 427 N.Y.S.2d 828 (1st Dep't 1980); Lombardo v. Doyle Dane & Bernbach, 58 A.D.2d 620, 396 N.Y.S.2d 661 (2d Dep't 1977).

9.   *Brinkley* at 12.

10.   *Id.* at 13, 14.

11.   *Id.* at 9, 15.

12.   Brief for Defendants-Respondents Elite Model Management Corp. and John Casablancas, p. 21.

Court Unravels *Agatha's* Publicity Mystery

Cases concerning the right of publicity continue to provide new and interesting law. One such decision relates to a motion picture and a book, each entitled "Agatha."[1]

Both the movie and book deal with an episode in the life of the world famous mystery writer Dame Agatha Christie. In December, 1926, Mrs. Christie, then married to Colonel Archibald Christie, disappeared from her home in England. Despite much publicity given to the disappearance and a major effort to find her, she remained absent for 11 days. To this day, her whereabouts during the 11 day period and the reason for Mrs. Christie's disappearance are a mystery.

Defendants Casablanca Record and Filmworks, First Artist Corporation and Warner Brothers Inc. commenced production of a motion picture and defendant Ballantine Books was involved in the publication of a book which presented a fictionalized account of what had occurred during the 11 day period. In each instance, Mrs. Christie is portrayed as an emotionally unstable woman who, during her disappearance, engaged in a sinister plot to murder her husband's mistress in an attempt to regain the alienated affections of her husband.

Claiming infringement of right of publicity and unfair competition, plaintiffs Rosalind Christie Hicks, (Mrs. Christie's sole legatee), Agatha Christie, Ltd. and William Collins Sons & Co., Ltd. (her assignees) moved to enjoin defendants from distributing the movie and the book. Defendants moved to dismiss plaintiffs' claims for failure to state claims on which relief could be granted.

In its decision, the Court first discussed the *Factors* case[2] in which it was held that the right in the publicity value of one's name or likeness is a valuable property right which is transferable and capable of surviving the death of the owner; provided that the owner "exploited" the right during his or her lifetime. In dicta, the Court wrote:

13

"While the *Factors* opinion does not define 'exploitation,' it would appear that a party claiming the right must establish that the decedent acted in such a way to evidence his or her own recognition of the extrinsic commercial value of his or her name or likeness, and manifested that recognition in some overt manner, e.g., making an *inter vivos* transfer of the rights in the name, . . . or posing for bubble gum cards . . ."

The court determined that Mrs. Christie had exploited her name during her lifetime because she had assigned rights to her literary works, bequeathed similar rights by testamentary disposition and entered into contracts for the use of her name during her lifetime in connection with movies and plays based on her books. Accordingly, her right of publicity survived her death and was properly transferred to the plaintiffs as her heirs and assignees.

The Court then turned to the question of whether the right of publicity attaches when one's name or likeness is used in connection with a book or a movie. In the opinion of the Court:

"The question is novel in view of the fact that more so than posters, bubble gum cards, or some other such 'merchandise,' books and movies are vehicles through which ideas and opinions are disseminated and, as such, have enjoyed certain constitutional protections not generally accorded 'merchandise.' It is complex because this Court is unaware of any other cases presenting a similar fact pattern or similar constitutional question with respect to this issue of right of publicity."

For guidance, the court examined cases involving the right of privacy under Section 51 of the New York Civil Rights Act, and concluded that the same exemptions from invasions of that right which are engrafted upon the privacy statute are engrafted upon the right of publicity. These exemptions include certain privileged uses of news, history, biography, and other factual subjects of public interest in which there appear necessary references to the names, portraits, identities or histories of living persons.

However, the Court rejected the contention of the defendants that the book and movie were each a protected biography because it found them to be fiction, not biography.

As fictionalizations, were the book and movie entitled to any constitutional protection? Applying a balancing test between society's interest in the speech for which protection is sought and the societal, commercial or governmental interests seeking to restrain such speech, the Court found that the movie and novel should be protected and that there are no countervailing legal or policy grounds against such protection.

In support of this position, cases involving Warren Spahn[3] and the University of Notre Dame[4] were cited.

The *Spahn* case involved the distribution of a book which was presented by the defendants therein as being a biography of the well-known baseball player Warren Spahn. However, in the book there were deliberate falsifications of events represented to be true, manufactured dialogue and erroneous statistical data.

In deciding that plaintiff's right of privacy in that case was violated, the Court of Appeals stated:

"We hold in conformity with our policy of construing sections 50 and 51 so as to fully protect free speech, that, before recovery by a public figure may be had for an unauthorized presentation of his life it must be shown, in addition to the other requirements of the statute, that the presentation is infected with material and substantial falsification . . . or with a reckless disregard for the truth. . ."

"To hold that this research effort [on the part of the author] entitled the defendants to publish the kind of knowing fictionalization presented here would amount to granting a literary license which is not only unnecessary to the protection of free speech but destructive of an individual's rights, albeit a limited one in the case of a public figure, to be free of the commercial exploitation of his name . . . ."

The *Notre Dame* case involved the distribution of a movie which satirized modern day events, people and institutions, including a football team identified as that of Notre Dame. The Appellate Division, in denying plaintiff relief pursuant to the New York Civil Rights Act and on grounds of unfair competition, stated:

"Motion pictures, as well as books, are a 'significant medium for the communication of ideas'; their importance 'as an organ of public opinion is not lessened by the fact that they are designed to entertain as well as to inform'; and like books, they are a constitutionally protected form of expression notwithstanding that 'their production, distribution and exhibition is a large-scale business conducted for private profit' . . . ."

The Court concluded that the *Spahn* case should be limited to its facts and that the *Notre Dame* case should govern. In the *Notre Dame* case, it was found that the defendant had not represented the events in the movie to be true and that a viewer of the film would certainly know the circumstances involved therein were fictitious. The Court then stated:

"It is clear from the review of these two cases that the absence or presence of deliberate falsifications or an attempt by a defendant to present the disputed events as true, determines whether the scales in this balancing process, shall tip in favor of or against protection of the speech at issue. Since the cases at bar are more factually similar to the Notre Dame case, i.e., there were not deliberate falsifications alleged by plaintiffs, and the reader of the novel in the book case, by the presence of the word 'novel,' would know that the work was fictitious, this Court finds that the first amendment protection usually accorded novels and movies outweighs whatever publicity rights plaintiffs may possess and for this reason their complaints must be dismissed.

Accordingly the Court finds that the right of publicity does not attach here, where a fictionalized account of an event in the life of a public figure is depicted in a novel or a movie, and in such novel or movie it is evident to the public that the events as depicted are fictitious."

It thus appears that in a situation involving the right of publicity, the following questions may be pertinent:

1. Did the decedent exploit the right during his or her lifetime?

2. What is the subject matter in which the person's name or likeness appears (e.g., book, movie, merchandise)?

3. Is the work factual or fictional?

4. If the work purports to be factual, are there distortions of fact?

5. If the work is fictional, is it clear to the public that it is a work of fiction?

FOOTNOTES

1. Hicks v. Casablanca Record and Filmworks, 464 F. Supp. 426 (S.D.N.Y. 1978).

2. Factors Etc., Inc. v. Pro Arts, Inc., 579 F.2d 215 (2d Cir. 1978), *cert. denied*, 440 U.S. 908 (1979).

3. Spahn v. Julian Messner, Inc., 21 N.Y.2d 124, 286 N.Y.S.2d 832 (1967), *appeal dismissed.*, Julian Messner, Inc. v. Spahn, 393 U.S. 1046 (1969).

4. University of Notre Dame DuLac v. Twentieth Century-Fox Film Corp., 22 App. Div. 452, 256 N.Y.S.2d 301 (1976).

Moot Court Competition Analyzes Right of Publicity

The hypothetical case of *Media Communications of America, Inc. v. Vets for Justice,* argued in the final round of the National Moot Court Competition, posed several questions relating to the existence and survival of and limitations on the right of publicity.

The facts of the case were as follows: Plaintiff Media Communications of America, Inc. ("Mecca"), a corporation in the fictitious State of Whittier involved in movie production, book publishing and other communications-related activities, sought an injunction in the United States District Court for the Southern District of Whittier enjoining defendant Vets for Justice ("Vets") from manufacturing, selling or otherwise distributing any buttons, posters, T-shirts or other items bearing the name or likeness of John Richmond. Richmond (a fictitious person) had served as a helicopter pilot in Vietnam and had received wide publicity in the press for his heroic conduct during the evacuation of Saigon in 1975. Shortly after his return from Vietnam, Richmond signed a contract with Mecca granting Mecca the exclusive right to "use, exploit and promote" his name and likeness "in any manner as fully and completely as Richmond could or might have used, exploited or promoted same, absent this agreement," for which Mecca paid Richmond $75,000.

In late 1978, Mecca produced "ARMAGEDDON THEN," an epic motion picture on the Vietnam War. Mecca asked Richmond to play himself in several short segments of the motion picture, but illness prevented him from doing so. In his place, Mecca used a professional actor, Val Lee, who resembled Richmond. In addition, portions of the original news photos depicting the evacuation of Saigon were incorporated into the film.

Richmond died in March, 1980. The following month, the film was released and was an immediate box office success. The surprise star of the film was Val Lee; although he only appeared in a few sequences, his portrayal of Richmond appealed to the American

19

public. According to Mecca's affidavit, "Apparently, the recent death of the handsome young war hero, Richmond, just prior to the release of the movie, created a cult of hero worshippers similar to that which followed the death of James Dean."

Mecca thereupon invested over $1 million in manufacturing posters, buttons, T-shirts, toys and games bearing either a picture of Val Lee in his role as Richmond or an "ARMAGEDDON THEN" scene depicting Richmond's heroic acts, to be sold in theater lobbies and retail stores. Mecca also spent an additional $1 million on nationwide advertising of these items. In two and one-half months, Mecca sold more than $500,000 worth of Richmond memorabilia. Sales steadily increased until defendant Vets began selling buttons and posters bearing Richmond's photograph over the word "Remember" outside theaters showing the film. Thereafter, sales declined approximately 25 percent.

In July, 1980, Mecca sued Vets, seeking injunctive relief based upon Vets' alleged misappropriation of Mecca's exclusive right of publicity in Richmond's name and likeness.

In opposition to Mecca's motion, Vets submitted the affidavit of Richmond's widow, Jean, a member of the Board of Directors of Vets, a not-for-profit corporation formed in May, 1980 under the laws of the State of Columbia to promote the interests of Vietnam veterans and their families. Vets planned to sue the federal government for injuries allegedly suffered by veterans due to their exposure to a chemical defoliant sprayed over the Vietnamese countryside. Jean Richmond alleged that if her husband had known about the injurious effects of this defoliant, which she believed to have been responsible for her husband's death, he would never have allowed his name to be associated with "ARMAGEDDON THEN."

In May, 1980, Jean Richmond donated various photographs of John, from the family album, to Vets for use in manufacturing buttons and posters to publicize Vets' cause and to raise money to support Vets' legal battle against the government. Vets contended that as of May, 1980, the publicity surrounding Richmond had long since subsided. According to Vets, between late 1975 and the date of his death in 1980, he was not the subject of any media reports.

In opposing Mecca's motion, Vets relied upon a 1945 decision of the Supreme Judicial Court of the State of Whittier and an unreported 1977 Whittier trial court opinion, both of which refused to recognize a right of publicity under Whittier law. Vets also asserted that any rights which Mecca might have obtained terminated upon Richmond's death, and that Vets' sale of Richmond memorabilia was protected under the First Amendment.

The United States District Court for the Southern District of Whittier concluded that it was not bound by the Whittier decisions which had refused to recognize a right of publicity in that state. The court held that the right of publicity is a clearly recognized property right which Richmond attempted to exploit during his lifetime by contracting with Mecca and which survived Richmond's death. However, the District Court denied Mecca's motion upon the ground that Vets' sale of memorabilia was "protected speech under the First Amendment."

The United States Court of Appeals for the Thirteenth Circuit unanimously affirmed the decision of the District Court, but on different grounds than those relied upon below. The Circuit Court held that under *Erie*[1] the federal courts were bound by the existing substantive law of Whittier as evidenced by the two Whittier state court decisions which did not recognize a right of publicity in that state. The circuit court also noted that "the likeness and name of John Richmond are in the public domain, and, except for restrictions imposed by the federal copyright statute, are available for all to use." The appeals court declined to reach the other issues presented.

The United States Supreme Court granted Mecca's petition for a writ of *certiorari* and this was the posture in which the case was presented to the contestants in the Moot Court Competition.

A basic issue presented in the case concerned the existence of a "right of publicity" and its survival after death. The common law right of privacy protects against interference with a person's "right to be left alone." That right has been said to encompass four distinct torts: intrusion; placing the plaintiff in a "false light"; public disclosure of embarrassing private facts; and misappropriation of the plaintiff's name or likeness for a commercial purpose. In nearly all jurisdictions, the right of privacy has been held to be personal to the individual and accordingly to be extinguished at death.[2]

The "right of publicity," by contrast, has been considered to be a right in the nature of a property right rather than a tort. The phrase was first used in a Second Circuit decision in 1953 which stated that:"We think that, in addition to and independent of [the] right of privacy (which in New York derives from statute), a man has a right in the publicity value of his photograph . . .

"This right might be called a 'right of publicity.' . . ."[3] A substantial majority of decisions since then have held that a right of publicity exists under appropriate circumstances.[4]

In the course of the Moot Court arguments, counsel for Vets argued that commercial exploitation of the name and likeness of a deceased person during his lifetime is a necessary condition for survival of the right. In a case involving the merchandising of material bearing Elvis Presley's name and likeness, the Second Circuit affirmed the grant of an injunction to an exclusive licensee following Presley's death, noting the right was exploited during Presley's lifetime.[5] Counsel for Mecca, however, cited cases holding that *inter vivos* exploitation is not necessary to survival of the right.[6] Mecca also argued that, in any event, Richmond exploited his right of publicity during his lifetime by entering into the exclusive contract with Mecca and by submitting to interviews and making television appearances.

Counsel for Vets contended that "only those who earn their livelihood from exploiting their attributes in some commercial manner, and who contract for such exploitation during their lives, possess an inheritable right."[7] Vets also cited the majority opinion in the *Lugosi* case,[8] which used a trademark analysis to conclude that Bela Lugosi had not, during his lifetime, used his name or likeness as Dracula so as to impress a secondary meaning on any business, product or service.

Counsel for Mecca cited the decision holding that the production of the play "A Day in Hollywood / A Night in the Ukraine" infringed the right of publicity of the Marx Brothers, which survived their death. The court stressed the finding that "the Marx Brothers exploited their rights of publicity in their self-created characters" during their lifetimes.[9] (This decision has been reversed on other grounds.) Counsel for Vets responded that the court in that case, as in another case in which a performer imitated Elvis Presley's appearance, dress and performing style in a live performance,[10] emphasized that the conduct that was found to be infringing appropriated significant portions of the plaintiff's act or character without contributing anything of value to society and was thus distinguishable.

With respect to the question of descendibility, several courts have characterized the right of publicity as a form of property right, on the ground that the protection against misappropriation of the commercial value of one's name and likeness is a form of property.[11] Counsel for Mecca argued that most forms of property are devisable; therefore, the right of publicity should likewise be devisable and should not terminate upon death.[12]

In addition, some commentators have suggested that the right of publicity is primarily analogous to copyright and accordingly should survive the death of the individual.[13] Counsel for Mecca reasoned that because rights to exploit fictitious characters are protected by copyright and, under the current Copyright Act, survive the death of the author, there is no logical reason why similar rights to exploit the name and likeness of an actual person should terminate upon death.

Counsel for Vets contended that the right of publicity is more closely analogous to the right of privacy, from which it was initially derived. As noted above, the right of privacy has generally been deemed a personal right which is not assignable and terminates at death.[14] Vets also argued that a claim for infringement of the right of publicity is analogous to a claim for injury to reputation. The right to recover for defamation, for example, has been held to terminate upon death.[15]

Some courts have premised their conclusion that the right of publicity is descendible on the ground that such survival is necessary as an incentive for an individual's "investment in the commercial development of the use of his personality."[16] Counsel for Vets in response cited a Sixth Circuit decision[17] in which the court held, contrary to the decision of the Second Circuit in a similar case,[18] that the right of publicity in Elvis Presley's name and likeness was not descendible. In its opinion, which rejected arguments that "making the right of publicity inheritable would . . . significantly inspire the creative endeavors of individuals in our society,"[19] the Sixth Circuit acknowledged that the Tennessee state courts had not decided the descendibility question. The court noted that if the right of publicity were held to be descendible, questions would arise as to how long the property interest in such a right should last, and at what point it would be considered to conflict with the right of free expression guaranteed by the First Amendment.

After the Sixth Circuit decision was issued in 1980, the Second Circuit reexamined the same question in a related case involving Elvis Presley and held that it was bound to defer to the Sixth Circuit's interpretation of this question with respect to transactions in Tennessee.[20] Since then, however, a lower Tennessee court has held that the right of publicity of the bluegrass singer, Lester Flatt, survived his death.[21]

Counsel for Vets also claimed that the right of publicity should not apply to "military heroes whose fame was gained on the public payroll"[22] and that the right should be "limited . . . to situations in which the individual earns at least part of his livelihood from the publicity that is to be protected."[23] Vets also argued that federal copyright law should preempt any common law right of publicity which Mecca may have, by analogy with Supreme Court cases holding that under the Supremacy Clause a state's unfair competition law could not prohibit the copying of an article not entitled to be protected under federal patent law.[24]

The fact pattern of the hypothetical case raised the further question of whether Vets' conduct was privileged under the First Amendment, even if the Court should decide that a descendible right of publicity exists.

Counsel for Vets argued that by analogy with the right of privacy, which has been held to be limited by the First Amendment,[25] "so too must the 'right of publicity' bow where such conflicts with the free dissemination of thoughts, ideas, newsworthy events, and matters of public interest."[26]

Counsel for Mecca cited the Supreme Court's decision in *Zacchini v. Scripps-Howard Broadcasting Co.,*[27] in which the Court held that a television station's broadcast of plaintiff's entire fifteen second human cannonball act was not protected by the First Amendment. Counsel for Vets countered that Zacchini should not bar a First Amendment defense because it involved the plaintiff's entire act and his ability to earn a living, and also because the plaintiff in that case did not seek an injunction but only sought payment for his act.

Several cases have focused on the medium in which a communication is expressed in determining whether such communication is protected by the First Amendment. Counsel for Vets cited a decision holding that a poster of Pat Paulsen which was commercially distributed during his satirical campaign for the Presidency was protected.[28] The court in that case stated that a medium embodying written words or pictures, including posters and handbills, would be protected in connection with the dissemination of news or public interest presentations.[29]

Counsel for Mecca referred to cases holding that a memorial poster of Elvis Presley was not protected by the First Amendment[30] and cited decisions holding that media such as motion pictures and books "are vehicles through which ideas and opinions are disseminated and, as such, have enjoyed certain constitutional protections, not generally accorded 'merchandise'"[31] or "commercial products."[32] Mecca thus argued that the posters, buttons and T-shirts at issue were not entitled to constitutional protection.

Counsel for Vets contended that its memorabilia bore not only Richmond's photograph, but also the message "Remember," which constituted a "unique or new" element that contributed to public debate and thereby was entitled to First Amendment protection.[33] Vets also claimed that its memorabilia amounted to "symbolic speech" protected by the First Amendment.[34] Counsel for Mecca responded that Vets' selling of its memorabilia outside theaters showing "ARMAGEDDON THEN" evidenced a commercial motivation[35] and that Vets could disseminate its political views by other means that would not infringe upon Mecca's rights.

FOOTNOTES

1.   Erie Railroad Co. v. Tompkins, 304 U.S. 64 (1938).

2.   In New York, the right of privacy is statutory and is codified in New York Civil Rights Law, Sections 50 and 51. The statutory right is not descendible. Frosch v. Grosset & Dunlap, Inc., 75 A.D.2d 768, 427 N.Y.S.2d 828 (1st Dep't 1980).

3.   Haelan Laboratories, Inc. v. Topps Chewing Gum, Inc., 202 F.2d 866, 868 (2d Cir.), cert. denied, 346 U.S. 816 (1953).

4.   See, e.g., Price v. Hal Roach Studios, Inc., 400 F. Supp. 836 (S.D.N.Y. 1975).

5.   Factors Etc., Inc. v. Pro Arts, Inc., 579 F.2d 215 (2d Cir. 1978), cert. denied, 440 U.S. 908 (1979); see Hicks v. Casablanca Records, 464 F. Supp. 426, 429 (S.D.N.Y. 1978).

6. Price v. Hal Roach Studios, Inc., *supra; see* Lugosi v. Universal Pictures, 25 Cal. 3d 813, 160 Cal. Rptr. 323, 603 P.2d 425, 447 (1979) (dissenting opinion).

7. Felcher & Rubin, *The Descendibility of the Right of Publicity: Is There Commercial Life after Death?*, 89 Yale L.J. 1125, 1131 (1980).

8. *See* note 6 *supra.*

9. Groucho Marx Productions, Inc. v. Day & Night Co., 523 F. Supp. 485 (S.D.N.Y. 1981), *rev'd*, 689 F.2d 317 (2d Cir. 1982).

10. Estate of Elvis Presley v. Russen, 513 F. Supp. 1339, (D.N.J. 1981).

11. *See, e.g.,* Cepeda v. Swift & Co., 415 F.2d 1205 (8th Cir. 1969); Haelan Laboratories, Inc. v. Topps Chewing Gum, Inc., *supra.*

12. *See* Price v. Hal Roach Studios, Inc., *supra,* 400 F. Supp. at 844.

13. Felcher & Rubin, *supra; see* Zacchini v. Scripps-Howard Broadcasting Co., 433 U.S. 562, 573 (1977); Lugosi v. Universal Pictures, *supra,* 603 P.2d at 446 (Bird, C.J. dissenting).

14. New York Civil Rights Law, Sections 50, 51; Lugosi v. Universal Pictures, *supra,* 603 P.2d at 430; Lombardo v. Doyle, Dane & Bernbach, Inc., 58 A.D.2d 620, 396 N.Y.S.2d 661 (2d Dep't 1977).

15. Wender v. Hamburger, 393 F.2d 365 (D.C. Cir. 1968).

16. Factors Etc., Inc. v. Pro Arts, Inc., 579 F.2d 215 (2d Cir. 1978), *cert. denied*, 440 U.S. 908 (1979); *see* Felcher & Rubin, *supra*, 89 Yale L.J. at 1128.

17. Memphis Development Foundation v. Factors Etc., Inc., 616 F.2d 956 (6th Cir. 1980), *cert. denied*, 449 U.S. 953 (1980).

18. Factors Etc., Inc. v. Pro Arts, Inc., *supra* note 5.

19. 616 F.2d at 959.

20. Factors Etc., Inc. v. Pro Arts, Inc., *supra* note 16.

21. Commerce Union Bank v. Coors, 7 Med. L. Rptr. 2204 (1981).

22. Memphis Development Foundation v. Factors Etc., Inc., *supra*, 616 F.2d at 959.

23. Felcher & Rubin, *supra*, 89 Yale L.J. at 1130.

24. *See, e.g.,* Sears, Roebuck & Co. v. Stiffel Co., 376 U.S. 225

(1964), *and* Compco Corp. v. Day-Brite Lighting, Inc., 376 U.S. 234 (1964).

25.   Spahn v. Julian Messner, Inc., 21 N.Y.2d 124, 286 N.Y.S.2d 832 (1967), *appeal dismissed*, Julian Messner, Inc. v. Spahn, 393 U.S. 1046 (1969).

26.   Rosemont Enterprises, Inc. v. Random House, Inc., 58 Misc.2d 1, 6, 294 N.Y.S.2d 122, 129 (Sup. Ct. N.Y. Co. 1968), *aff'd*, 32 A.D. 2d 892, 301 N.Y.S.2d 948 (1st Dep't 1969); Hicks v. Casablanca Records, *supra*, 464 F. Supp. at 430.

27.   433 U.S. 562 (1977).

28.   Paulsen v. Personality Posters, Inc., 59 Misc. 2d 444, 299 N.Y.S.2d 501 (Sup. Ct. N.Y. Co. 1968).

29.   299 N.Y.S.2d at 506.

30.   Factors Etc., Inc. v. Pro Arts, Inc., *supra* note 5; Factors Etc., Inc. v. Creative Card Co., 444 F. Supp. 279 (S.D.N.Y. 1977).

31.   Hicks v. Casablanca Records, *supra*, 464 F. Supp. at 430.

32.   Guglielmi v. Spelling-Goldberg Productions, 25 Cal. 3d 860, 160 Cal. Rptr. 352, 603 P.2d 454, 463 (1979) (Bird, C.J. concurring).

33.   Felcher & Rubin, *Privacy, Publicity, and the Portrayal of Real People by the Media*, 88 Yale L.J. 1577, 1601-05 (1979).

34.   *See, e.g.*, Spence v. Washington, 418 U.S. 405 (1974); Tinker v. Des Moines Independent Community School District, 393 U.S. 503 (1969).

35.   *See* Zacchini v. Scripps-Howard Broadcasting Co., *supra*, 433 U.S. at 581 (Powell, J., dissenting); Presley v. Russen, *supra*, 513 F. Supp. at 1359.

The Controversial *Bindrim* Decision

Producers of theatrical and television motion pictures based upon events in the life of a real person frequently have depicted that person fictionally to obtain insulation from a lawsuit. The effectiveness of such protection, always questionable, has been buffeted by the controversial *Bindrim* decision.[1]

There, a California Appellate Court upheld a jury's verdict awarding Paul Bindrim, a licensed clinical psychologist, damages against Doubleday and Gwen Davis Mitchell, the publisher and author, respectively, of a book entitled "Touching."

Bindrim had employed the technique of a so-called "nude marathon" in group therapy as a means of helping people shed their psychological inhibitions with the removal of their clothes. Mitchell attended these sessions (after agreeing in writing that she would not write articles based upon what transpired) and then entered into a contract with Doubleday to write a book which depicted a nude encounter session in Southern California led by a "Doctor Simon Herford."

Bindrim complained that he was libeled by the devastating manner in which his counterpart, Herford, was depicted in that novel. In particular, he cited a passage of the book describing a session in which Herford tried to convince a minister that the minister's wife should attend the nude marathon. Bindrim claimed he never used the vulgar language which Herford employed in this passage and, in fact, a transcript of the actual session derived from a tape recording made at the time supported Bindrim's contention.

Of particular note in this case was the fact that the author went to great lengths to fictionalize the character of Herford. In the novel, Herford was described as a "fat, Santa Claus type with long white hair, white sideburns, a cherubic rosy face and rosy forearms" while Bindrim was clean shaven and had short hair.

However, the Court rejected the claim of the defendant that, even if there were libelous statements in the novel, there was no showing

29

that Bindrim was identified as the character Herford. Three witnesses, all of whom had participated in or observed one of Bindrim's nude marathons, testified at the trial that they "recognized" Bindrim as the fictitious Dr. Herford. The dissenting opinion stated that the only characteristic mentioned by any of those three witnesses as identifying Bindrim was the nature of the therapy practice. The majority opinion disagreed, concluding that, other than the difference in physical appearance and the fact that Herford was a psychiatrist rather than a psychologist, the character Herford was very similar to the actual plaintiff, and thus Bindrim and Herford were one.

Bindrim was libeled, the decision stated, notwithstanding that he admittedly was a public figure. As such, under the law of libel there must be a showing of actual malice by the defendant before a judgment may be had against her. Mitchell, by virtue of her "reckless disregard for the truth" of what transpired at the encounter session, was found by the jury to have possessed actual malice. The decision also indicated that what constitutes malice must be determined on a case by case basis.

The opinion also rejected the claim of the defendants that because the book was labeled as a "novel," Bindrim could not claim that the characters in the book were factual representations of real persons rather than fictional characters. Whether a reader identifying Bindrim with Herford would regard the passages complained of as mere fictional embroidering or the reporting of actual language and conduct was a question for the jury, and here the Appellate Court refused to overturn the verdict of the jury against the defendants.

That the decision is a complex and somewhat confusing one is indicated by the dissent to the opinion written by the presiding justice and the additional opinion written by an associate justice concurring with the majority opinion and explaining why the dissent was incorrect.

A writer or producer who wishes to depict fictionally a real person must tread carefully. In the absence of obtaining releases, he must take care to avoid both possible invasion of that person's privacy and libelous depiction of him. Unfortunately, specific guidelines in close situations may sometimes be lacking; for, as noted in the Bindrim decision, each case must be judged on its own facts.

FOOTNOTES

1.   Bindrim v. Mitchell, 92 Cal. App.3d 61, 155 Cal. Rptr. 29 (1979), *cert. denied*, 444 U.S. 984 (1979).

Variety, October 24, 1979

The *Springer* Case: Libel and Fiction

For the past few years the *Bindrim* decision[1] has been the subject of controversy and concern among authors, publishers and producers. A recent decision[2] indicates that the impact of the *Bindrim* case for suits brought in New York may not be as far reaching as once suggested.

The facts in the case are concisely stated in the opinion of the Court:

"Plaintiff and defendant Tine, the author of the novel in question, attended Columbia University from 1974 to 1978. They met and a close personal relationship developed. In 1978 Tine completed the draft of *State of Grace*, a novel dealing with Vatican finances and politics. Plaintiff and Tine discussed the plot during the volume's hatching stage and plaintiff, at Tine's request, reviewed the book for editorial purposes. Indeed, Tine informed plaintiff that he had loosely patterned the relationship between the hero, the papal private secretary, and the heroine, an investigative reporter and the daughter of one of Italy's most influential and powerful industrialists, on the relationship between them.

"Plaintiff and Tine terminated their friendship in 1978, apparently with some rancor. In 1980 *State of Grace* was published by defendant, the Viking Press. Chapter 10 of the book, which covers some 10½ pages, depicts the origin of and one evening in the relationship between the Italian industrialist, described as 'the cossack of Italian business, ruthless and demanding,' and his mistress, Lisa Blake. Although brief, the chapter is most explicit about their sexual exploits."

In an affidavit taken of Springer in 1981, she contended that Tine was motivated by "a vicious attempt to avenge his bruised ego" after the termination of their three year relationship. She also charged that after the novel's publication Tine had "asked me how I liked the book and my role in it. When I replied negatively, Mr. Tine stated that I had better get used to it as his second book was scheduled for publication in September of 1981 . . . and that I was again the 'Lisa' in the book who was also to be depicted as a whore."

Tine, in his affidavit, denied Springer's contention that he had asked her to read his manuscript and stated that "Lisa Blake is not Lisa Springer nor is the portrayal of the fictional character Lisa Blake meant to signify any actual person at all. Lisa Blake is a fictional character created to show a side of the novel's protagonist not shown elsewhere in the book; she has not been created to hurt or injure anyone, including plaintiff."

Springer contended that the portrayal in the novel of Blake was actually a portrayal of her and that several people who knew both her and Tine and their relationship knew and understood Blake and plaintiff to be the same person. Accordingly, Springer brought an action to recover for the alleged libel contending that the depiction of Blake as a "whore" who engages in various types of abnormal sexual activity is defamatory of her.

Plaintiff's complaint set forth seven causes of action, three of which are relevant for discussion in this chapter.

Plaintiff's fifth cause of action alleged a violation of Sections 50 and 51 of the New York Civil Rights Law. The Special Term dismissed this cause of action stating that the fact that plaintiff's surname did not appear in the book rendered any possible claim for invasion of privacy under Section 51 of the Civil Rights Law fatally defective. In affirming, the Appellate Division cited several cases, including the well known action involving the motion picture "Dog Day Afternoon"[3] to support its conclusion that in New York there is no right of action for invasion of privacy independent of statute. Because neither the plaintiff's name, portrait or picture was used in *State of Grace*, the plaintiff has no cause of action under the Civil Rights Law.

Special Term had denied defendants' motion to dismiss the first two causes of action which were grounded in libel, noting that to maintain such an action it must appear that plaintiff is the person concerning whom the alleged defamatory statement was made. It is not necessary for the person actually to be named in the publication if the allusion is apparent. Special Term concluded that plaintiff established a sufficient connection with Lisa Blake to indicate that the derogatory characterization of Blake in Chapter 10 could be "of and concerning" Springer.

The Appellate Division disagreed. Stating that it is for the Court to decide whether a publication is capable of the meaning ascribed to it, the Appellate Division defined its task to include searching for similarities and dissimilarities in order to determine whether a person who knew plaintiff and who read the book could reasonably conclude that plaintiff was Lisa Blake.

The Court noted the following similarities between Lisa Springer and Lisa Blake: both had similar physical attributes; both had graduated from college and Blake once had lived on 114th Street, a street on which Springer had lived and still lives. The Court referred to these similarities as being in large part superficial, then noted that the dissimilarities between Springer and Blake, both in manner of living and in outlook, "are so profound that it is virtually impossible to see how one who has read the book and who knew Lisa Springer could attribute to Springer the lifestyle of Blake." The dissimilarities to which the Court referred were that: plaintiff is a tutor on the college level while Blake, described as a "whore," held the "title deed for a coop apartment in the Olympic Tower on Fifth Avenue" which was well-furnished but not overbearing; Blake received a "salary" of $75,000 and drove a BMW, and she lived luxuriously. No indication of Springer's manner of living was set forth except as the Court could infer it from the nature of her work.

The Court cited *Allen v. Gordon* (86 A.D.2d 514) in which there appeared in the book *I'm Dancing As Fast As I Can* references to a psychiatrist with the fictitious name of Dr. Allen. There was only one psychiatrist named Allen in the Manhattan phonebook and he sued for defamation. The Court held that the dissimilarities between the Dr. Allen named in the book and the plaintiff in that action were such as to negate any suggestion that he was the person indicated.

The Court also referred to *Giaimo v. Literary Guild* (79 A.D.2d 917) which held that "where the person defamed is not named in a defamatory publication, it is necessary, if it is to be held actionable as to him, that the language used be such that persons reading it will, in the light of surrounding circumstances, be able to understand that it refers to the person complaining."

Finally, the Appellate Division cited *Lyons v. New American Library, Inc.* (78 A.D.2d 723). There, plaintiff, the sheriff of Franklin County in New York who maintained his office at the County Seat in Malone, New York, brought suit because, in the novel *.44*, a fictional version of a detailed search by the New York City Police Department to discover the "Son of Sam" killer, a conversation among New York City police officers engaged in the investigation referred to the incompetence of a sheriff headquartered in Malone, New York. The decision in that case noted that "the work clearly states that it is fiction and that, combined with plaintiff's admission that he did not participate in the Son of Sam investigation, requires the conclusion that the passage is not actionable."

The Appellate Division concluded that "the teaching of these cases is that for a defamatory statement or statements made about a character in a fictional work to be actionable the description of the fictional character must be so closely akin to the real person claiming to be defamed that a reader of the book, knowing the real person, would have no difficulty linking the two. Superficial similarities are insufficient as is a common first name. In the circumstances here presented we cannot say that Chapter 10 of *State of Grace* is susceptible of the interpretation ascribed to it by plaintiff."

Judge Kupferman dissented and indicated that he would affirm the Special Term's rulings. Stating that the majority opinion had omitted and glossed over items of similarity which would indicate that the character of Lisa Blake referred to the plaintiff, Judge Kupferman reasoned that it cannot be determined as a matter of law that the writing is not "of and concerning" the plaintiff. He also noted that there can be no question that the portrayal in the book is defamatory and that the only issue is one of identification.

The dissent also cites a letter from Mrs. Nadine Gartner, a former lecturer and teacher at Columbia University who had known both plaintiff and defendant Tine, which contained the following paragraph:

"I have read Robbie's book and am absolutely amazed that *he has put Lisa into it—under her own name!—as a psychology student student who has become a high-class prostitute*. What a childish revenge! She is described making torridly clinical 'love' to an Italian tycoon-gangster who connives to have the Pope killed . . . I wonder if L. (Lisa) has read it?? (emphasis added)."

This letter was heavily relied upon by Plaintiff in her arguments to the Court.

Plaintiff has appealed this decision which, if upheld, will add to the body of New York law in regard to libel and fiction and perhaps diminish to some extent the effect of the *Bindrim* decision.

FOOTNOTES

1.   Bindrim v. Mitchell App., 92 Cal. App.3d 61, 155 Cal. Rptr. 29 (1979), *cert. denied*, 444 U.S. 984 (1979).

2.   Springer v. Viking Press, No. 14809 (N.Y. Sup. Ct. App. Div. First Dept. December 14, 1982).

3.   Wojtowicz v. Delacorte Press, 43 N.Y.2d 858, 403 N.Y.S.2d 218 (1978).

Chapter Two
Names, Credit and Titles

Motion Picture Titles and the Lanham Act

It is well settled that the title of a motion picture neither is covered by the copyright in the picture nor subject to copyright protection. Because the title often is a valuable element of the picture, producers and their attorneys welcome any development which adds to the scope of protection afforded to the title. One such development is the decision of a U.S. District Court in *Brandon v. The Regents of the University of California.*[1]

Liane Brandon was an Assistant Professor of Film Production and Media Studies at the University of Massachusetts. An experienced filmmaker, having been involved with several motion picture shorts which had been widely distributed, she produced, directed, and edited in 1970-1971 an eight minute black and white film entitled "Anything You Want To Be" ("plaintiff's film"). The Court described plaintiff's film as follows:

"Anything You Want To Be . . . by Liane Brandon. . . identifies the conventional self-image instilled in women as well as the stereotyped roles they are forced into. A high school girl is shown being continuously frustrated as she tries to make independent choices regarding her future. She wants to be class president, but ends up as secretary instead. She visits her guidance counselor to discuss her desire to become a doctor, and comes out dressed in nurse's attire. Chemical instruments are mysteriously transformed into kitchen utensils as she tries to use them, and a book on political history she wants to read is surreptitiously replaced by a cookbook. At every step, the alternatives to the traditional female roles seem to disappear and the girl's aspirations are foiled. Despite the seriousness of its theme, this film's approach is light, even humorous, and it is particularly valuable for use with junior and senior high school audiences."

Distribution of plaintiff's film commenced in 1971 and during the period of 1971 through 1977 was handled by three different companies. Catalogues, brochures, mailing circulars and other materials widely advertising and promoting the film were distributed and

41

reviews were published in books, magazines, professional journals and newspapers. In addition, plaintiff's film was exhibited at several important film festivals and institutional exhibitions and received a Blue Ribbon at the American Film Festival in 1972. All of the foregoing was of relevance to the Court in its finding that the title of plaintiff's film was well-known and identifiable to persons who would purchase, rent, and exhibit films dealing with women's rights and sex-role stereotyping.

The defendant, through its Extension Media Center ("EMC") was engaged in the business of selling and renting its catalogue of approximately 3,000 films throughout the United States and in foreign countries. In the summer of 1972, in response to a growing demand for films about women, EMC formed a special committee to evaluate existing films. The plaintiff's was among the films which the committee recommended be purchased by EMC. On May 15, 1973 EMC wrote to plaintiff inquiring whether it could purchase a print of plaintiff's film for rental use. On both May 17, 1973 and June 19, 1973 plaintiff wrote to EMC confirming her refusal to sell a print. In May of 1974, EMC again attempted to purchase a print of plaintiff's film, this time by submitting an order to one of plaintiff's distributors. Again EMC's bid was rejected.

In 1974, the director of EMC travelled to Far West Laboratory for Educational Research and Development ("Far West") to view three short films dealing with sex-role stereotyping produced by Far West employees. One of these films entitled "Anything They Want To Be," copyrighted in the name of Far West, was allegedly conceived by a Far West employee. In comparing this film with plaintiff's film, the Court stated that the former:

". . . was seven rather than eight minutes long, addressed the same issue of sex-role stereotyping in intellectual and career-oriented activities, and treated the experiences of several, rather than a single, high-school girls. Moreover, scenes in the Far West film are quite reflective of scenes or dialogue in plaintiff's film. Scenes in the Far West film, for example, question whether a girl can become a fireman, a chemist, or a doctor; the identical occupations are portrayed or mentioned in plaintiff's film."

In May of 1974, EMC agreed to underwrite the remaining production costs of the Far West film in exchange for exclusive distribution rights thereto. The Far West film was delivered to EMC by October, 1974 (though the production-distribution agreement between EMC and Far West was not executed until August 28, 1975). EMC then commenced distribution of the film, advising the public of its availability through a press release and a subject matter description published in its bulletin, its film catalogue and its advertising brochures. On September 11, 1975, plaintiff sent written demand to EMC asking that EMC stop distribution of the film under the title "Anything They Want To Be." EMC did not do so.

Thereafter plaintiff commenced a civil action under the Lanham Act (15 U.S.C.A. Section 1125(a)(1970)) and a two day non-jury trial ensued, following which, on plaintiff's motion and pending the Court's decision, the Court entered a preliminary injunction enjoining EMC from exhibiting, selling, renting, leasing, distributing, or transferring any prints of the disputed film and from publishing or distributing any catalogue or similar advertising or promotional material referring to the film.

The decision of the Court noted that: "Plaintiff has not alleged any violation of federal copyright law but has charged defendant with: (1) the deliberate, intentional copying of the title, subject matter and theme of plaintiff's film in order to trade on its excellent reputation; (2) unfair competition; and (3) false description and representation by defendant's use of the title of plaintiff's film in interstate commerce."

In evaluating the testimony of witnesses for the defendant at the trial the Court found much of it to be not credible and specifically found that in August of 1973, the producers of defendant's film "in a brazen act of outright plagarism, deliberately selected the title 'Anything They Want To Be' . . . in order to trade upon the reputation and goodwill of plaintiff's similarly titled film."

In discussing the applicability of the Lanham Act, the opinion stated:

"In ruling the plaintiff has proved a case under 15 U.S.C.A. Section 1125(a), I have in mind that the offending Far West film clearly constitutes 'goods' and admittedly has traveled in interstate commerce. Although the title of copyrighted work is not absolutely protected against use by others, *Warner Bros. Pictures v. Majestic Pictures Corp.,* 70 F2d 310, 312 (2d Cir. 1934), a film title, nevertheless, is entitled to judicial protection under the common law doctrine of unfair competition (as codified in Section 1125 (a)) when it has attained a 'secondary meaning,' i.e., when it is associated in the minds of a substantial number of people with the goodwill that that particular film has achieved through public distribution and advertising. *Warner Bros. v. Majestic Pictures Corp.,* supra; *National Picture Theatres, Inc. v. Foundation Film Corp.,* 266 F. 208, 210-11 (2d Cir. 1920). I find and rule that the plaintiff's widely- and well-known film had acquired the requisite 'secondary meaning' in at least the eyes of the film-consuming public.

"I further rule that the existence of this secondary meaning for the title and the greatly confusing similarity between the two films amply establish that defendant's conduct in distributing the Far West film with a plagiaristic title supports branding defendant's conduct as the use of a 'false description or representation' in connection with goods placed in interstate commerce. I rule that the findings of a decrease in plaintiff's income from her film concurrent with the increase in defendant's income from the Far West film proves the actual damages caused by defendant's use of the misleading title. It should be noted that it is sufficient to establish a violation of Section 1125(a) to show that the title used created a false impression. *John Wright, Inc. v. Casper Corp.* 419 F. Supp. 292, 325 (E.D. Pa. 1976).

"I am persuaded that plaintiff has proved each of the essential elements of a cause of action under 15 U.S.C.A. Section 1125(a) and that EMC's distribution of the Far West film under the title 'Anything They Want To Be' constituted and constitutes unfair competition, entitling plaintiff to all relief available under Section 1125(a). Because of the abundant evidence of defendant's three unsuccessful attempts to purchase prints of plaintiff's film for EMC rental and because of [EMC's] prior knowledge, I find that defendant acted deliberately with an awareness of the similarity of titles, subject matter, theme, presentation, running time, and price range of both films before it entered into the Distribution Agreement. Because of this deliberate pirating of plaintiff's property, I rule that plaintiff is entitled to injunctive relief, damages and an accounting, and the preliminary injunction previously entered herein shall now issue as a permanent injunction enjoining defendants from any further distribution of the film 'Anything They Want To Be' under the title or any other title similar to 'Anything You Want To Be.' Defendant will be directed to give notice in all its catalogues or in response to any inquiries for the film 'Anything They Want To Be' that the film is no longer available from EMC and that plaintiff's film is available from New Day Films."

The Order also provided that plaintiff was entitled to an accounting of all of defendant's gross income from the sale and rental of the Far West film and, in an unusual decision, ordered that defendant be entitled to recover reasonable attorneys' fees and costs.

The applicability of the Lanham Act to a film title has been hailed by some as a landmark decision and dismissed by others as relatively inconsequential. The significance of this opinion will become apparent as further decisional law appears.

FOOTNOTES

1.   Brandon v. Regents of the University of California, 441 F. Supp. 1086 (D. Mass. 1977).

Protection for "A Little Romance"

Protection again has been afforded a plaintiff with an interest in a motion picture title.[1] The suit was brought by Orion Pictures Company, Inc., the distributor of a motion picture entitled "A Little Romance" against Dell Publishing Co. Inc. the publisher of a paperback version of the book upon which the motion picture was based and which bore the same title as that motion picture.

In 1977 a book by the French author Patrick Cauvin entitled $E = MC^2$, *Mon Amour* achieved considerable popularity in Europe. Orion decided to produce and distribute a film based upon the book and obtained the agreement of Pan Arts Associates, Inc. to acquire motion picture rights to the book and to prepare a screenplay based on it. A principal of Pan Arts, the noted director George Roy Hill, was to direct the motion picture.

When Dell learned in late 1977 of the plan to produce a movie based upon $E = MC^2$, *Mon Amour*, it entered into an agreement with the French author and his publisher to obtain the English translation and paperback publication rights for the book. Dell bought the right to market the book under any title it desired but, according to its editorial director, intended from the beginning to use the same title for the book as would be used for the movie.

Shortly thereafter representatives of Dell and Orion attempted to negotiate a tie-in relationship between the release of the book and the movie. In August, 1978, after Orion informed Dell that it intended to release the movie under the title "A Little Romance" Dell advised its employees that it would publish the book under the same title.

Because director Hill concluded that as a result of substantial rewriting, the screenplay for the movie was dissimilar from the original book, Orion elected in early 1979 not to go forward with the proposed tie-in agreement. Orion offered as an alternative to allow Dell to publish a novel based upon the screenplay, but Dell, having already spent $25,000 to obtain the rights to the original work as well as having a royalty obligation to the author (which it feared

47

already spent $25,000 to obtain the rights to the original work as well as having a royalty obligation to the author (which it feared might be breached by the sale of a new literary work derived from the screenplay) rejected this offer. Accordingly, Orion and Dell did not enter into a tie-in arrangement.

The opinion of the Court described what next happened:

"Despite the lack of any agreement, Dell, apparently in the belief that Orion had no protectable interest in the title or in the publicity that the movie would generate, went forward with the publication of its paperback under the title *A Little Romance*. The defendant also chose to include on the front cover of the book the pronouncement that it was 'NOW A MAJOR MOTION PICTURE,' along with a drawing of three people who bore noticeable resemblances to Laurence Olivier and the two child stars of the picture (with the Eiffel Tower and Paris in the background). Dell's publicity releases sent to potential wholesalers and retailers of the book rested heavily upon the movie tie-in, commenting that the movie, considering its director and stars, 'is sure to receive intense promotion and publicity —that's bound to help the Dell book!—the release of the major film will boost sales of this translation of a greatly acclaimed French novel'."

After Dell had distributed 125,000 copies of the book throughout the United States and Canada, Orion moved for a preliminary injunction restraining Dell from using the title "A Little Romance" and from unfairly competing with it. The complaint alleged that Dell violated Section 368-d of the New York State General Business Law and the common law standard for unfair competition. Orion also sought an order directing Dell to reacquire and destroy all copies of the book previously published and delivered.

Stating that the relative rights of the parties cannot be assessed in a vacuum, the Court compared the book with the movie and, after promulgating its critical evaluation of each, concluded that the movie was substantially different from, and better than, the book. Noting that the proper legal result would not be self-evident from its critical analysis of the works, the Court then evaluated plaintiff's claim that defendant deliberately sought a "free-ride" on the millions of dollars plaintiff was spending on advertising and that the publication and distribution of the paperback book would diminish the popularity of the movie.

The Court determined that to be protected by the laws of unfair competition, the title must have attained some secondary meaning (i.e., it has come to be associated in the minds of a substantial number of people with a certain type of film produced by a particular individual and thus protected from use by others).

Rejecting the claim of Dell that because it marketed its book before the movie opened, no secondary meaning in the title could have developed, and thus no unfair competition could have occurred, the opinion noted that even if a work has not been released, a sufficient amount of pre-release publicity of the title may cause the title to acquire recognition sufficient for protection. In this regard, the opinion cited Metro-Goldwyn-Mayer, Inc. v. Lee[2] in which it was found that as a result of an extensive advertising campaign, the film title "The Wonderful World of the Brothers Grimm" had been publicized sufficiently to achieve a secondary meaning, even though the film itself was at that time uncompleted.

Further, the Court pointed to defendant's own promotional literature and advertising indicating that Dell was counting on the plaintiff's publicity as the primary means by which to promote the sale of the book. Such an attempt to "pass off" by the defendant has been held not only as evidence of likelihood of confusion, but also of secondary meaning as well.

Further, the Court indicated that there appeared to be growing support for the proposition that a secondary meaning "in the making" should be protected, at least to the extent of preventing intentional attempts, as by the defendant in the instant case, to capitalize on the efforts and good will of others.

The Court then determined that under Section 368-d of the New York State General Business Law relief is not limited to situations in which the plaintiff has proved a secondary meaning in a mark or a title. Rather, the controlling question in determining whether there had been a State law violation is "whether the acts are fair or unfair, according to principals recognized in equity."[3]

Having determined that the title was sufficiently identifiable with plaintiff's film to be entitled to protection, the Court next addressed the question whether there was any likelihood that an ordinarily prudent purchaser would be misled as to the source of the goods in question. The opinion indicated that such a person would be likely to assume that the book bore a very close resemblance to the movie, especially in light of the inscription "NOW A MAJOR MOTION PICTURE" on the cover. Dell's book, by virtue of its title and inscription, gives the impression that it is the official novel version of the movie and therefore highly similar in content to it. In promoting such an impression, Dell had misled the public.

Factors to be considered in determining the relief to be afforded were the bad faith of the defendant in adopting the plaintiff's title and artwork and the overstating of the relationship between the film and the book. In granting injunctive relief, the Court concluded that the effect of the infringement and unfair competition was neither determinable nor compensable by money damages.

It was virtually impossible to recapture the books already in the hands of retailers and the reading public. Consequently, the injunction which was issued prohibited the defendant from using on subsequent printings of the book the title, artwork or other representations which stated or implied a greater relationship between the two works than actually existed. Further, defendant was ordered to revise its promotional material to indicate the actual relationship between the book and the movie.

FOOTNOTES

1.   Orion Pictures Co., Inc. v. Dell Publishing Co. Inc., 471 F. Supp. 392 (S.D.N.Y. 1979).

2.   212 Cal.App. 2d 23, 27, Cal.Rptr. 833 (Dist. Ct. App. 1963).

3.   Santa's Workshop, Inc. v. Sterling, 282 App. Div. at 329-30, 122 N.Y.S.2d at 499.

Screen Credit and the Lanham Act

When a person's screen credit is omitted from a production, the damage may be substantial but the remedies few. As a result of a federal court decision[1] it appears that a potential remedy may be found in the Lanham Act.

The decision involved Richard Perin who was engaged to render services as executive producer of the television series "For You . . . Black Woman."

Perin claimed that he was instrumental in selecting the hostess and set designer of the series, establishing budgets and schedules, determining guests, hiring a line producer and director and assisting in locating potential sponsors.

He also claimed that he was promised orally, and received in all programs of the series broadcast during the first year, credit as executive producer. This credit also appeared in newspaper articles and promotional materials.

During the production of programs in the first year, Ms. Saint Charles Lockett represented one of the sponsors, and in such capacity, participated in the decision-making process which affected the way in which the programs ultimately appeared on the air.

After production had been completed of 12 of the 22 programs for the second year (six had to be reshot for technical reasons), the producers of the programs terminated Perin's services, claiming that he had failed to render effective services and that he was engendering dissension among the production staff.

The producers claimed that following the date of Perin's termination, Ms. Lockett took up the performance of the functions which Perin previously had performed. Perin claimed that her role in the second year did not differ from hers in the first.

The dispute between Perin and the producers arose when Perin received no credit on the programs broadcast during the second year and Ms. Lockett received credit as "Executive In Charge of Production."

Perin brought a suit requesting that the broadcast of the programs be enjoined. After two days of hearings, the request was denied.

Also, Perin filed a complaint based on the Lanham Act in which, among other things, he sought money damages.

The Lanham Act makes liable to a civil action any person who uses in connection with goods or services, or containers for goods or services, a false designation of origin or a false description or representation, and allows any person who believes that he is likely to be damaged by such false description to bring suit.

Ordinarily the Lanham Act is thought of as an act involving trade names and trademarks, and the defendants in the Perin action made that argument, stating that the Act does not apply to the issuance of screen credit.

Perin claimed that the Act did apply when, as in his case, there was a false and unjustifiable attribution of screen credit to someone at the expense of another, so as to imply that the former person is the author of an important work performed and accomplished by the latter.

In his papers Perin cited the *Brandon* case in which the Lanham Act was the basis for protection of a motion picture title and also furnished to the Court a substantial amount of evidence regarding the significance of screen credit.

Although the *Perin* case was settled before a trial, it is of significance because of the refusal of the judge to dismiss Perin's claim. In effect, the Court upheld a claim based upon the Lanham Act in an instance when there may have been a false attribution of screen credit.

The decision was rendered orally by the judge; no written opinion will be issued. It should be noted that the case involved an unusual set of circumstances and that there was no decision based upon the merits of the parties' respective claims. However, because the decision was rendered by a highly regarded court and because it indicates the growing importance of the Lanham Act in entertainment litigation, it is of great interest.

FOOTNOTES

1.   Perin Film Enterprise v. Two Productions, 400 P.T.C. Journ. (10-19-78) A-13 (S.D.N.Y. 1978).

Variety, April 11, 1979

Give Credit Where Credit Is Due

When a jury awarded damages for breach of contract and punitive damages in a California case involving the failure of a producer to furnish to a television actor the credit set forth in his agreement, the defendants made a motion for a judgment notwithstanding the verdict and for a new trial. The decision of the judge denying those motions has been upheld on appeal.[1]

Plaintiff, William Smithers, had signed a deal memo with MGM dated January 29, 1976 regarding the television series entitled "Executive Suite." Paragraph 4 of that memo provided that plaintiff would receive credit "on the end titles as a Co-Star in alphabetical order, on a crawl." Paragraph C.12(c) of that memo further provided that "except for the parts of Don Walling, Helen Walling and Howard Rutledge, this deal is on a Most Favored Nation Basis, i.e., if any other performer receives greater compensation than Artist (Smithers), Artist shall receive that compensation. Additionally, no other performer shall receive more prominent billing or a better billing provision than Artist (except with respect to where his name is placed alphabetically on the credits.)"

From the inception of the television broadcasts of the series, the three named actors playing the parts mentioned in the above provision received "Star Billing" and were seen before the commencement of each episode of the series in a scene which identified them by name with the word "Starring" preceding the scenes. However, from the beginning of such broadcasts, a fourth member of the cast, playing a role which was not specified in the Most Favored Nation provision of the memo, also received such "Star Billing." Smithers never received equal Star Billing, but rather received "Also Starring" billing which, in this instance, meant that Smithers' name was shown with the names of other actors in rapid succession at the conclusion of each episode of the series.

Smithers alleged that after he notified MGM on or about December 2, 1976 that he wished MGM to honor the contractual rights concerning billing, he not only was advised through a representative of MGM that his request was denied, he also was requested by MGM that he release it from its contractual obligation as specified in Paragraph C.12(c) of the memo and allow it to elevate several members of the cast receiving "Also Starring" billing to "Star Billing," excluding Smithers from such billing. Smithers refused this request and alleged that he was told by a representative of MGM on or about January 5, 1977 that the changes in such billing nevertheless had been effectuated. Smithers further contended that the president in charge of MGM Television Production informed Smithers' agent that if Smithers persisted in demanding his contractual rights he would not likely work again for MGM nor for CBS.

In a letter to the attorney for Smithers, the associate general counsel of MGM categorically rejected Smithers' statement that MGM or any of its representatives ever threatened Smithers or told him that MGM would not employ him in the future because of the credit dispute. MGM further denied that it materially breached any of its obligations to Smithers and stated that "even assuming we have committed a technical breach (which we deny), we are convinced that Mr. Smithers will not be able to prove any damages." Finally, in that letter, MGM indicated that it found the attitude of Mr. Smithers regarding the credit dispute "uncooperative" and "somewhat unbelievable" in that MGM and CBS "have tried to revamp a television show which was in ratings trouble and, during this difficult period, we have kept everyone advised of our plans."

Thereafter, Smithers instituted suit against Columbia Broadcasting System, Inc., Metro-Goldwyn-Mayer, Inc. and certain named individuals setting forth the following causes of action:

First: Seeking a declaration that plaintiff was entitled to receive Star Billing in future episodes of the series on television, theatrically and in any and all re-runs of the episodes whenever and wherever in the world they may be shown. Such a determination purportedly was necessary to prevent the loss to plaintiff of the unique advantage of Star Billing which he had bargained for and which loss directly affects plaintiff's future, both professionally as to his status in his profession and the quality of roles which will become available to him, and economically as to the salary which he will be able to demand.

Second: For breach of contract which breach, plaintiff alleged, caused him to suffer a severe loss to the detriment of his professional career and future earning power.

Third: For tortious breach of contract and a breach of the implied covenant of good faith and fair dealing. Among the actions cited by plaintiff in this cause of action were MGM's attempts to obtain plaintiff's permission for billing changes when MGM already knew that the changes were effectuated and the exploitation by the president of MGM's television production arm of his position of greater bargaining power over the plaintiff by threatening him with the loss of future employment opportunities with MGM and with CBS if Smithers persisted in demanding equal billing stature with his fellow performers in the series. (As noted in the opinion of the Court, apparently the threat was not carried out as Smithers continued employment on the series and also was employed thereafter by MGM. Nor was it shown that the threat ever was communicated to CBS). As a result of such breach, plaintiff alleged the loss of a vital asset to his future earning power and severe mental anguish and distress.

Fourth: For fraudulent deceit. In this regard, plaintiff alleged that when defendants made the promise set forth in Paragraph C.12(c) of the memo, they knew it to be false and it was made with the intent to induce Smithers to act in the series.

Fifth: For intentional infliction of emotional distress. This cause of action was later dismissed.

Sixth: For interference by CBS with contractual rights. This cause of action also was dismissed.

After trial, the jury awarded damages as follows: on the cause of action for breach of contract—$500,000; on the cause of action for breach of the implied covenant of good faith and fair dealing— $300,000; on the cause of action for fraud—$200,000; and punitive damages in the amount of $2 million.

Defendants then made a motion for a judgment notwithstanding the verdict and for a new trial. On August 21, 1981 the Court denied defendants' motion for judgment notwithstanding the verdict, denied defendants' motion for a new trial on condition that plaintiff accept certain reductions of damages and issued a memorandum specifying reasons for reducing certain damages.

In regard to the award of damages for breach of contract and the award of damages for breach of covenant of good faith, the Court held that the evidence was sufficient to support the jury's verdict and that the amount awarded was not excessive. As to the award of damages for fraudulent deceit, the Court reduced the award of the jury to one dollar because that award duplicated the award of damages for breach of contract and breach of covenant of good faith. In so doing, the Court cited its instructions to the jury in fixing the damages for fraud: "The amount of such an award shall be an amount which will compensate him for profits or other gains which might reasonably have been earned by virtue of the star billing had the plaintiff been given such billing by the defendants" and "reasonable compensation for any pain, discomfort, fears, anxiety and other emotional distress suffered by the plaintiff and for similar suffering reasonably certain to be experienced in the future from the same cause." The Court indicated that these two items of damages were virtually the same as those covered in the second and third causes of action and that although the evidence supported a verdict for fraudulent deceit and there was actual damage, in order to prevent double recovery the verdict should be reduced to a nominal amount.

The Court indicated that the award for punitive damages was excessive, even though the defendants were guilty of both tortious breach of contract and fraud. "The defendants took advantage of their superior economic position to threaten the plaintiff with loss of future employment, not only with their company, but also as to the CBS network television. (sic.) Furthermore, the testimony . . . fully supported the conclusion that the conduct of the defendants was 'extreme and outrageous' . . . Defendants' fraud prevented plaintiff from advancing his professional career in which he, admittedly, had already achieved a respected position. It could have cost defendants little to live up to their contract, but instead, they chose to use the heavy hand of threatened economic punishment to achieve their own way. For all these reasons, an award for punitive damages is justified but in a lesser amount than $2,000,000." Taking into consideration the adequate award of compensatory damages by the jury for breach of contract and breach of covenant of good faith and considering the nature of defendants' conduct, its effect upon the plaintiff together with consideration of the wealth of the defendant MGM and by way of deterrents and punishment, the Court elected to reduce the award for punitive damages to $1 million.

The Court conditioned the denial of the motion for a new trial and for judgment notwithstanding the verdict on plaintiff's consenting to the Court's reduction of damages as aforesaid. Plaintiff agreed to such a reduction.

This decision of the Court was affirmed by the California Court of Appeals for the Second Appellate District.

This case continues the trend which has developed towards protecting earned or bargained for credit.

FOOTNOTES

1.   Smithers v. Metro-Goldwyn-Mayer, Inc., California Superior Court, No. C 18778 (August 21, 1981), *aff'd*, 189 Cal. Rptr. 20 (2d Dist. 1983).

Protecting the Group Name

The name of a performing group may be a highly valuable commercial asset, and the ownership of that name often is the subject of controversy. When litigation occurs, courts must balance public policy questions, such as deception of the public or misrepresentation, against legal theories including trademark, contract, corporate and partnership law.

These disputes almost invariably involve groups which have attained some measure of success, as it is public recognition that invests the group name with its commercial value. For example, by using a name which is the same as or similar to the name of a well-known group, as in *Five Platters, Inc. v. Purdie,* where a new group called itself "The Fabulous Platters" and "The New Century Platters" and performed in a style similar to the "Platters,' " a well-known group which had sold millions of records, a new group might be "able to obtain more and better employment."[1]

Similarly, in *Marshak v. Green,*[2] plaintiff, the manager of a group known as "The Drifters" and the owner by assignment of the service-mark registration of the name, succeeded in enjoining a departed member of the group from using the name; the court found that "[d]efendants in promoting their own group were thus trading on the name and good will of plaintiff's group." One of the defendants admitted he had selected the name "The Drifters" for the new group because the " 'only thing that draws is a name that is well-known or half-way known or whatever,' and 'The Drifters' is such a name."

Frequently issues of group name ownership develop when a group has disbanded or has undergone changes in the composition of its members. Ideally, these questions of ownership would always be governed by agreements among group members, but often this is not the case, and other areas of law come into play.

In *Noone v. Banner Talent Associates, Inc.,*[3] plaintiff Peter Noone, former lead singer of the popular English group known as "Herman's Hermits," brought suit under Section 43(a) of the Lanham Act (115

U.S.C. Section 1125(a)) against the other members of the group and their non-exclusive booking agency to enjoin them from using the group name in the United States several years after Noone had left the original group to pursue his own career. The Lanham Act provides in pertinent part that any person who affixes a false designation or representation in connection with any goods or services and causes such goods or services to enter into commerce, is liable to a civil action by any person who believes he is or may be damaged by the use of such false description or representation. No agreement existed among the group members of "Herman's Hermits" as to ownership of the name and Noone argued that the use of the name was a "false description" in that "Herman" was no longer a member of the group. The court denied the defendant's motion to dismiss, holding that "Section 43(a) provides relief against the type of unfair competition that is analogous to misappropriation of trade names. . . . If the name 'Herman's Hermits' has acquired a sufficient secondary meaning to imply, even now, that plaintiff is the lead singer of the group, then the use of the word 'Herman's' would be misleading and give rise to an action under Section 43(a) as a false description."[4] The court similarly allowed plaintiff's claim of unfair competition.

An agreement among group members can be significant in resolving competing claims to a group name, as is evident in *Gutkowski v. Jeckell*.[5] There, plaintiffs obtained a preliminary injunction against defendants' use of the name, "1910 Fruit Gum Company," in connection with defendants' advertising and performances. Prior to defendants' departure from the group, plaintiffs and defendants had entered into an express agreement providing that plaintiffs would have the ownership and exclusive right to use the group name and the right to substitute new members in the event any of the group members departed.

Occasionally, however, courts will accord greater weight to public policy considerations, such as the public's right to know, than to contractual arrangements among group members. In the early case of *Messer v. the Fadettes*,[6] an orchestra leader organized a band of musicians which she named the "Fadette Ladies Orchestra." She subsequently assigned to plaintiff all her "right, title and interest in and to the organization . . . together with all right acquired in the establishment, name and trademark in the words 'Fadette Ladies

Orchestra.' " At the time of plaintiff's suit, no members of the original orchestra remained, and the court held that any right to the trade-name was personal to the original orchestra leader, and could not be assigned. The court found further that any use by plaintiff of this trade-name would serve to "defraud and mislead" the public by implying that plaintiff "and such musicians as she employed were the same persons who had formerly gained a good reputation under this name. It is well settled that the courts will not enforce a claim of this kind, which contains a fraud upon the public."[7]

Similarly, in *Fuqua v. Watson*[8] the court narrowly interpreted an agreement among three surviving members, and the executrix of the fourth member's estate, of the group known as "The Ink Spots." The agreement precluded one survivor, Watson, from using the group name at all, and granted the right of use to the other two survivors, Kenny and Fuqua. When Fuqua and his new group, which did not include Kenny, brought an action to restrain Watson from using the name, the court held that any right to the name resided only in the joint venture of Fuqua and Kenny, and not in either of them individually. The court then challenged the legality of the joint venture's ownership of and right to use the name: "The name 'Ink Spots' . . . achieved international fame and became known and associated in the eyes of the general public and in the entertainment world with that of the four original members of the groups . . ." Upon the death of one of the members, the joint venture or partnership terminated and the group with which the name was associated "ceased to exist." The commercial value of the name derived from "the personal skills of the four original members of the vocal group and, therefore, could not be truthfully used by others after this group disbanded . . . Thus, when plaintiffs advertise their group as the 'Ink Spots,' they are, in effect, perpetrating a fraud upon the public by such misrepresentation."[9]

Differing in some respects from the *Messer* and *Fuqua* decisions are the cases involving the corporation formed by the group known as "The Platters." The corporation, Five Platters, Inc., was formed in 1956 by the five original members of the group, and was the sole and exclusive owner of the name, "The Platters," as well as the service-mark registration for the name. Gradually all original members of the group departed, and were replaced by new members.

Departing members were granted the limited right to bill their performances as a person "formerly of the Platters."

In *Five Platters, Inc. v. Purdie*, the plaintiff corporation was found to be entitled to compensatory and punitive damages, as well as injunctive relief against further use by defendants of names such as "The Fabulous Platters." The court found that a strong secondary meaning and "valuable good will" had attached to the name, and found further, in apparent contradiction to the *Messer* and *Fuqua* findings, that plaintiff "has not misrepresented to the public the composition of its singing group and, in particular, plaintiff has not misrepresented to the public that its singing group was composed of the same or some of the same persons who were members of the group when it first attained national recognition and popularity in the 1950s."[10] Thus, defendants were found to be in violation of Section 43(a) of the Lanham Act and were held liable for their intentional use of the name and their attempts to "cause confusion and to mislead and deceive the consuming public" by indicating that their group was composed of former members of the Platters and by promoting a similar style of performance to that of the original group.

In *Five Platters, Inc. v. Cook*,[11] the Platters' corporation, which had been found entitled to injunctive relief against the defendant's performances under the names of "Tommy Cook and The Sounds of The Platters" and the "Platters," filed for the lifting of a suspended six month sentence against defendant. The court found that the defendant had in fact violated the injunction and imposed the suspended sentence for other earlier violations of the injunction—six months imprisonment.

The issues of ownership of and the right to use a group name are of great importance not only to the group members but also to certain third parties, such as record companies, which expend time and money in the development and promotion of groups and their records. Agreements between a record company and an artist often will provide that the company is granted the exclusive right to use and to license the use of the artist's name during the term of the agreement for phonograph record purposes. These agreements also may provide a warranty that the use of such name will not infringe the rights of any third party. Among the record company's primary concerns are that the company not expend large sums of money in promoting a group only to find, first, that the promotion of the group by its group name infringes on some third party's rights to that name and, second, that these sums of money have been expended in a way that assists a group which may be commercially competitive with its own group.

Anderson v. Capitol Records Inc.[12] deals with a conflict between the rights of a record company which expended large amounts of money in promoting an English group known as "Flash" and the rights of a popular performing group in the San Francisco area of California, which had not commercially released any albums, and which also was known as "Flash." The California group, which had been performing under the name "Flash" for three and one-half years prior to the arrival of the English group, obtained a certificate of registration of the name in California, and sought to enjoin Capitol's use of the name, claiming service-mark infringement and unfair competition. The court found that the "name 'Flash' had come to mean plaintiff's group to a substantial number of rock music fans in the San Francisco Bay area," that the name had acquired a secondary meaning in that area, and that ". . . there is a justifiable inference that deception or confusion will result." In fashioning its relief, the court took into account Capitol's expenditures which were in excess of $250,000, as well as plaintiff's localized rights in the name. Thus, the court limited the relief to "requiring that defendant distinguish the British group's business, music or services sufficiently to avoid deception or confusion," and enjoined Capitol from using the name "Flash" for any purpose by itself in connection with the sale, distribution, or promotion of any records, albums, or tapes in the Bay area. The court further enjoined the sale of records, albums, or tapes of the British "Flash," "unless one or more other words are used in connection with said name 'Flash' in such way as to clearly, explicitly and readily identify the music as that of the group from England," and these identifying words had to appear on the package as well as on the record or tape. Finally, Capitol was obligated to advise disc jockeys in the area to identify "Flash" as the English group when playing their music on the radio.

There may be no guarantee for a successful solution to the problems rising in the area of group names, but at the least, an agreement should be drafted among group members covering all aspects of their internal relations, including the replacement and substitution of members, ownership of the group name, and the right of departed members to be billed as former members of the group. Although, because of the public deception issues noted above, the legal effect of an outright transfer of a group name to a new or different group is unclear, some attempt at "self-regulation by contract will be superior to leaving the matter at large to decision-makers who may not like the sound of music."[13]

FOOTNOTES

1.   Five Platters, Inc. v. Purdie, 419 F. Supp. 372, 381 (D. Md. 1976).
2.   505 F. Supp. 1054, (S.D.N.Y. 1981).
3.   398 F. Supp. 260 (S.D.N.Y. 1975).
4.   *Id.* at 263.
5.   NYLJ, Nov. 25, 1968, p. 16. col. 4.
6.   46 N.E. 407 (Sup. Jud. Ct. Mass. 1897).
7.   *Id.* at 407.
8.   107 U.S.P.Q. 251 (Sup. Ct. N.Y. Co. 1955).
9.   *Id.* at 252.
10.   Five Platters, Inc. v. Purdie, 419 F. Supp. at 386.
11.   491 F. Supp. 1165 (W. D. Pa. 1980).
12.   178 U.S.P.Q. (Cal. Super. Ct. 1973).
13.   Spiegel, I., "Rights in Group Names," *Performing Arts Review,* at pp. 423-24.

Chapter Three
Copyright Protection

Hurdles in Copyright Litigation

Courts frequently are called upon to adjudicate disputes in which the plaintiff claims that a motion picture or television producer has made unauthorized use of his work. These actions most often are based on allegations of copyright infringement and unfair competition. Because the potential financial rewards of a successful production are quite high, such lawsuits abound despite the numerous obstacles which the plaintiff must overcome in order to prevail.

The initial and perhaps greatest difficulty confronting a plaintiff in such a copyright infringement action is in the dichotomy between the unprotectible idea and its protectible expression. In keeping with the concept that no monopoly exists over ideas, the protection in the Copyright Act for "original works of authorship" extends only to the "expression of [an] idea—and not to the idea itself.[1] Unfortunately, no clear test exists which defines "when an imitator has gone beyond copying the 'idea,' and has borrowed its 'expressions.' Decisions must therefore inevitably be ad hoc."[2]

The courts have attempted to define certain standards, based on the "substantial similarity" of the works, to determine whether infringement of the expression exists. Although the standards remain vague, it is clear that the similarities which must exist to result in a finding of infringement require more than mere similarities in theme; rather a finding of substantial similarities of detail, scenes, events and characterizations is necessary. According to Judge Learned Hand in *Nichols v. Universal Pictures Corp.*,[3] "[u]pon any work . . . a great number of patterns of increasing generality will fit as more and more of the incident is left out. The last may be no more than the most general statement of what the [work] is about . . .; but there is a point in this series of abstractions where they are no longer protected, since otherwise the playwright could prevent the use of his 'ideas,' to which, apart from their expression, his property is never extended."

67

Plaintiffs in the case of *Giangrasso v. CBS, Inc.*[4] were unable to overcome this hurdle of proving substantial similarity of expression. Plaintiffs were the writers and owners of a copyrighted script, intended for possible television production. That script described a radio station and its disc jockey's remote broadcast from a local bank; gunshots are heard, a holdup and bank robbery unfold, the robber approaches the oblivious disc jockey and a humorous exchange follows in which the disc jockey attempts to interview the baffled robber as just another passerby. Plaintiffs alleged that an episode of defendants' television series, "WKRP in Cincinnati," infringed their copyrighted work. Defendants' script described the "hijacking" of a radio broadcast: an unemployed disc jockey in search of publicity draws a gun, holds up an on-location broadcast at a record store and takes over the broadcast.

The District Court compared the respective scripts in detail and found that any similarity between the scripts existed "only at a level of abstractions too basic to permit an inference that defendants wrongfully appropriated an 'expression' of plaintiffs' ideas. Furthermore, plaintiffs' characters are too undeveloped to permit protection . . ." The court found that plaintiffs' characters were primarily "types" with little development, and concluded that the lack of substantial similarity between the scripts and the characters warranted granting defendants' motion for summary judgment without a trial.

In *Warner Bros., Inc. v. American Broadcasting Companies, Inc.*, the plaintiffs, Warner Brothers, Film Export, A.G. and DC Comics, Inc., owners of the copyrighted motion pictures, television shows and comic books featuring Superman, were unsuccessful in three attempts[5] to obtain judicial relief against the production and exploitation of defendants' television series entitled, "The Greatest American Hero." The defendants' work featured a "hungry-looking, non macho young man" by the name of Ralph Hinkley who acquires super powers but, in a comedic vein, cannot control them.

Plaintiffs in *Warner Bros.* were unable to prove the requisite substantial similarity of expression necessary to obtain relief for copyright infringement. The works in question contained numerous attributes common to the two characters including super-strength, super-hearing, super-vision, super-speed, super-breath, invulnerability and the ability to fly. However, in view of the characters' costumes, personalities, histories and attitudes toward their super- powers, the works were not found to be substantially similar.

In granting defendants motion for summary judgment, the district court concluded that the "total concept and feel" of the works was different, and that "what defendants took from plaintiffs' works and incorporated into ['The Greatest American Hero'] were unpro- tected ideas. Chiefly, what was taken was the idea of a superhero who fights evil—a benevolent super-human." The district court con- cluded that the works in question were "insubstantially similar" as a matter of law and that the principal characters in each were "so dissimilar as to preclude a finding of substantial similarity."[6]

Plaintiffs fared no better with their claim of unfair competition. The court recognized that plaintiffs' enormous successes with their superhero character could well have catalyzed defendants' creation of superhero Ralph Hinkley, but held that "such encouragement, without more, is not actionable. A defendant is permitted to capi- talize on a market or fad created by another provided that it is not accomplished by confusing the public [into believing] that the prod- uct is the product of the competitor." The court thus granted sum- mary judgment on plaintiffs' unfair competition claim, finding that there was no likelihood of confusion between the works.

The doctrine of "scénes à faire," relied on to some extent in the opinion, represents another barrier to the plaintiff's ultimate victory in this area of infringement litigation. This doctrine provides that a "common idea is only capable of expression in more or less stereotyped form."[7] Certain stereotypical descriptions, events or characters will often flesh out a common theme, and these stereo- types may crop up in various works without providing the basis for a claim of copyright infringement. Thus, in *Jason v. Fonda*[8] defend- ants' motion to dismiss plaintiff's claim for copyright infringement was granted. Here, plaintiff alleged that the motion picture, "Coming Home," infringed plaintiff's copyrighted book entitled *Concomitant Soldier—Woman and War*. The court found that although both works "deal generally with subjects such as morality and the effects of war on women, injured veterans and soldiers, these ideas are not protectible in and of themselves," and found further that similarities between the works consisted of "the use of similar but unprotectible

ideas, of commonly cited historical facts, of sequences which necessarily follow from a common theme (scénes à faire), or of other
unprotectible characteristics."

Similarly, in *Alexander v. Haley*,[9] the court found that Alex Haley's *Roots* did not infringe plaintiffs' book, *Jubilee*. Both works dealt
with the subject of slavery, and the court opined that, given this
common subject matter, certain common themes, characters, settings and situations would necessarily emerge in both works, and
that their appearance in *Roots* did not constitute copyright infringement of *Jubilee*. (See p.73, for further discussion of the *Roots* case.)

Access, along with substantial similarity of expression, must be
established in order to prove copyright infringement. A defendant
must have had access, whether by actual reading or by knowledge,
to the plaintiff's work before unlawful copying can be shown. The
court in the *Jason* case found only a slim showing of potential access:
plaintiff's book had been published by a vanity press, and between
200 and 700 copies of the book were available through various
bookstores in Southern California. According to the court, this
measure of availability created no more than a "bare possibility"
of access by defendants to plaintiff's work.

In *Mann v. Columbia Pictures, Inc.*,[10] the Court of Appeals affirmed the trial court's judgment notwithstanding the verdict on
the grounds of lack of substantial similarity and lack of access, and
affirmed the overturning of a jury award to the plaintiff in the
amount of $185,000. Plaintiff had allegedly submitted a 29-page
format entitled *Women Plus* to defendant Columbia Pictures for
consideration as the basis for a motion picture. The format described
six central characters in a beauty salon setting, and outlined a
number of scenes emanating from the salon. Plaintiff claimed her
work constituted the basis for defendants' theatrical motion picture,
"Shampoo."

The court found first that plaintiff's "abstract ideas are not literary
property" and that defendants could use the "theme, plot, and ideas
contained in *Women Plus*," because no substantial similarity existed
between "Shampoo" and plaintiff's outline "as to form and manner
of expression, the portion which may be protectible property." The
court then found that the evidence was insufficient to establish
access, either through submission to the movie studio or through

contact between the screenplay writers of "Shampoo" and the individuals to whom plaintiff's outline was allegedly submitted.

The trend which appears in this area of copyright infringement litigation is that, for a number of reasons, it is the "defendant's game."[11] These reasons center around the above-noted difficulties of overcoming the idea-expression dichotomy, proving that a defendant's work is substantially similar in expression as well as in concept to the plaintiff's, doctrine of scénes à faire and the requirement that access to the plaintiff's work be proven. Other legal hurdles facing the plaintiff include the lack of copyright protection afforded to research and historical facts and the potential for independent creation of similar works. Further, the plaintiff faces the substantial out-of-pocket expenses involved in maintaining the action, which must be balanced against the customary insurance protection acquired by defendants against this type of claim. Accordingly, the prospective plaintiff and his attorney must examine carefully the merits of the case and the possibility of a sizeable recovery before proceeding in what has become a costly and difficult category of litigation.

FOOTNOTES

1. Mazer v. Stein, 347 U.S. 201, 217 (1954).
2. Peter Pan Fabrics, Inc. v. Martin Weiner Corp., 274 F.2d 487, 489 (2d Cir. 1960).
3. 45 F.2d 119, 121 (2d Cir. 1930).
4. 534 F. Supp. 472 (E.D.N.Y. 1982).
5. The plaintiffs first brought an action for a preliminary injunction, which was denied. 523 F. Supp. 611 (S.D.N.Y. 1981). They appealed the denial to the Second Circuit which affirmed in an opinion supporting virtually all of the lower court's findings of fact and conclusions of law. 654 F.2d 204 (2d Cir. 1981). On the eve of trial, after twice considering and denying a motion by defendants for summary judgment, the district court granted the motion. 530 F. Supp. 1189 (S.D.N.Y. 1982). That decision was *sub judice* before the Second Circuit at the time this book went to press (Docket No. 82-7152).

6.   In emphasizing the differences between the works, the first District Court opinion denying injunctive relief observed that "numerous differences tend to undercut substantial similarity." 523 F. Supp. at 616, citing Durham Industries, Inc. v. Tomy Corp., 630 F.2d 905, 913 (2d Cir. 1980) and Herbert Rosenthal Jewelry Corp. v. Honora Jewelry Co., 509 F.2d 64, 65 (2d Cir. 1974). On their appeal of that first decision, the plaintiffs argued that the district court incorrectly focused upon the differences rather than the similarities between the works. The Second Circuit disagreed, saying, "we . . . conclude that Judge Motley properly considered the great difference between the works in analyzing whether the parties works were substantially similar" (654 F.2d at 209).

7.   Reyher v. Children's Television Workshop, 533 F.2d. 84, 91 (2d Cir. 1977).

8.   526 F. Supp. 774 (1981), aff'd 698 F.2d 966 (1983).

9.   460 F. Supp. 40 (S.D.N.Y. 1978).

10.   178 Cal. Rptr. 500 (Ct. App. 1981).

11.   See Rosen, "Current Trends in Entertainment Litigation; the Insurance Empire Strikes Back," The Entertainment and Sports Lawyer 1 (1982).

The *Roots* Infringement Case

Authors and producers will be interested in a decision in a copyright infringement suit brought against both the author and publisher of the novel *Roots*.[1] That decision spelled out certain classes of written expression which are not afforded copyright protection.

The suit was instituted by Margaret Walker Alexander who had written a novel *Jubilee* and a pamphlet *How I Wrote Jubilee*. The former recounted the life of the author's great grandmother, Vyry, from her childhood (ca. 1835) and early adulthood in slavery, through the Civil War years and into Reconstruction. The latter told of the author's career, including her struggle to complete the novel and an explanation of certain matters contained in it.

In comparing the works, the court stated that *Roots* covered a much broader canvas than *Jubilee*. The narrative in *Roots* began about 1750 in Africa, then continued through multiple generations of a single family described as ancestors of the author Alex Haley, and through the birth and life of the author. Well over a fifth of the book was set in Africa and approximately three-quarters covered a period antedating the time of *Jubilee*.

The court agreed with the position of the defendants that Haley's work did not infringe upon the copyright of either of plaintiff's works. The decision classified Ms. Alexander's claimed infringements into several categories, then concluded that none of these categories were capable of copyright protection.

The first category included matters of historical or contemporary fact. In this connection, the court stated that no claim of copyright protection can arise from the fact that the plaintiff had written about historical and factual items, even if it were conceded that Haley was alerted to the facts in question by reading Jubilee.

The second category encompassed materials traceable to common sources, public domain or folk custom. A number of the claimed infringements were "embodiments of the cultural history of black Americans, or of both black and white Americans playing out the cruel tragedy of white-imposed slavery." When such common sources exist for the alleged similarity, or when the material is not original with the plaintiff, there is no infringement. This group of asserted infringements can be no more the subject of copyright protection than the use of the name of a president or a similar piece of historical information.

The third category included *scènes à faire*—incidents, characters or settings which, as a practical matter, are standard in the treatment of a given topic. Illustrative are attempted escapes, flights through the woods pursued by baying dogs and other events customarily found in stories depicting the miseries of slavery.

Also cited as a category were clichéd language, metaphors and the very words of which the language is constructed. Such methods of expression are not subject to copyright protection; nor are phrases and expressions conveying an idea that can only be, or is typically expressed in a limited number of stereotyped fashions. The court felt that the similarities of such words and expressions only demonstrated the use of obvious terms by both authors to describe expectable scenes.

It should be noted that the *Roots* decision only covered the applicability of the copyright protection to methods of written expression. There was no deviation from the accepted maxim that it is the method of expression, rather than the idea itself, which is capable of copyright protection.

FOOTNOTES

1. Alexander v. Haley, 460 F. Supp. 40 (S.D.N.Y. 1978).

Variety, November 1, 1978

Historical Facts Unprotected by Copyright

The decision of the United States District Court for the Southern District which granted summary judgment to the defendants in an infringement action relating to a work based upon an historical subject has been affirmed by the Court of Appeals.[1]

The litigation arose from three separate accounts of the last voyage and destruction of the Hindenburg. The first was a full-length book by A.A. Hoehling entitled *Who Destroyed the Hindenburg?* Published in 1962, the book was the result of Mr. Hoehling's study of investigative reports, previously published articles and books, and his interviews with survivors of the crash and others who possessed information about the Hindenburg. In the final chapter of his book, Hoehling suggests that all proffered explanations of the explosion, except for deliberate sabotage, are unconvincing. He concludes that the most likely saboteur was Eric Spehl, a rigger on the Hindenburg crew who was killed in the explosion.

Ten years later, defendant-appellee Michael Mooney, published his book, *The Hindenburg.* In the opinion of the Court, Mooney's endeavor could be categorized as more literary than historical in its attempt to weave a number of symbolic themes through the actual events surrounding the tragedy. Spehl is portrayed in Mooney's version as a sensitive artisan with needle and thread who ultimately plants the bomb that ignites the hydrogen and causes the devastating explosion.

Mooney acknowledged that he consulted Hoehling's book and relied on it for some detail. He claimed that he first discovered the "Spehl-as-saboteur" theory when he read a book entitled Wings of Mystery written by Dale Titler (ironically, Titler stated that he copied Hoehling's theory of sabotage in writing his book). Mooney also claimed to have studied the complete National Archives and *New York Times* files concerning the Hindenburg as well as all previously published material. He even claimed to have travelled to

Germany, and to have visited Spehl's birthplace and to have conducted a number of interviews with survivors.

Universal Pictures acquired the motion picture rights to Mooney's book and then commissioned a screenplay to be written based on it. In the film which eventually was produced, the actions of a rigger named Boerth are ultimately responsible for the destruction of the Hindenburg.

After extensive discovery was conducted in regard to the claim by Hoehling against Mooney and Universal based upon copyright infringement and common law unfair competition, the District Court granted defendants summary judgment.

In affirming the decision of the District Court, the Court of Appeals reasoned that to prove infringement, Hoehling must demonstrate that defendants "copied" his work and that they "improperly appropriated" his "expression." (There was no dispute that Hoehling had a valid copyright in his book.) Ordinarily, the question of substantial similarity is a close factual issue which results in the denial of summary judgment. However, the Court noted a series of copyright cases in the Southern District of New York which granted defendants summary judgment where all alleged similarities related to non-copyrightable elements of the plaintiff's work. The opinion cites these cases as signalling an important development in the law of copyright which permits courts to put a swift end to meritless litigation and avoid lengthy and costly trials. Drawing on these cases, the Court assumed both copying and substantial similarity among the works in question, but concluded that all similarities pertained to various categories of non-copyrightable material. By assuming substantial similarity, the Court eliminated the necessity to deal with the alleged instances of copying among Hoehling's work and defendants' book and motion picture.

Appellees argued that Hoehling's plot is an idea which is not copyrightable as a matter of law. Hoehling's rejoinder was that although ideas themselves are not subject to copyright protection, his expression of an idea is.

The Court noted that when dealing with works of fiction, the distinction between an idea and the manner in which it is expressed is especially elusive. But where, as in the instant case, the idea at issue is an interpretation of an historical event, the decisional law holds that such interpretations are not copyrightable as a matter of law. In citing a decision relating to a biography of Howard Hughes, the Court stated that although the plot of the two works in the *Hughes* case were necessarily similar, there could be no infringement because of the public benefit in encouraging the development of historical and biographical works and their public distribution.[2] To avoid a chilling effect on authors who contemplate tackling an historical issue or event, broad latitude must be granted to subsequent authors who make use of historical subject matter, including theories or plots. Then, quoting Learned Hand, the Court stated "there cannot be any such thing as copyright in the order of presentation of the facts, nor, indeed, in their selection."[3]

Because the hypothesis that Spehl destroyed the Hindenburg is based entirely on the interpretation of historical fact, such an interpretation, whether or not it originated with Mr. Hoehling, is not protected by his copyright and can be freely used by subsequent authors.

For this same reason, the claim by Hoehling that a number of specific facts, ascertained through his personal research, were copied by appellees also was denied. The cases decided in the Second Circuit make clear that factual information is in the public domain. Mooney and Universal each had the right to avail itself of the facts contained in the book and to use such information, whether correct or incorrect, in its literary work. Here, the Court rejected the holding in *Miller v. Universal*[4] (a decision which subsequently was reversed and now is in accord with the *Hoehling* decision) and stated that it refused to subscribe to the view that an author is absolutely precluded from saving time and effort by referring to and relying upon prior published material. It is just such wasted effort noted the Court, that the proscription against the copyright of ideas and facts is designed to prevent.

The Court was careful to note that in distinguishing between themes, facts and "scénes à faire" on the one hand and copyrightable expression on the other, the Court will not allow a wholesale usurpation of a prior author's expression. A verbatim reproduction of another's work, even in the realm of non-fiction, is actionable as a copyright infringement. In the instant case, it is clear that all three authors relate the story of the Hindenburg differently.

Concluding its analysis, the Court stated that in works devoted to historical subjects, a second author may make significant use of a prior work, so long as he does not bodily appropriate the expression of another. This principle is justified by the fundamental policy which underpins the copyright law—the encouragement of contributions to record knowledge. The "financial reward guaranteed to the copyright holder is but an incident of this general objective rather than an end in itself." Knowledge is expanded as well by granting new authors of historical works a relatively free hand to build upon the work of their predecessors.

FOOTNOTES

1. Hoehling v. Universal City Studios, Inc. and Mooney, 618 F.2d 972 (2d Cir. 1980), *cert. denied*, 449 U.S. 841 (1980).
2. Rosemont Enterprises, Inc. v. Random House, Inc., 366 F.2d 303 (2d Cir. 1966), *cert. denied*, 385 U.S. 1009 (1967).
3. Myers v. Mail & Express Co., 36 C.O. Bull. 478, 479 (S.D.N.Y. 1919).
4. Miller v. Universal City Studios, Inc., 460 F. Supp. 984 (S.D. Fla. 1978), *rev'd*, 650 F.2d 1365 (5th Cir. 1981).

Disney and the Air Pirates—Characters and Conjuring Up

Questions involving protection of characters and fair use were discussed in an opinion of the U.S. Court of Appeals for the Ninth Circuit.[1] That opinion resulted from a suit brought by Walt Disney Productions against The Air Pirates and others who prepared and published two magazines of cartoons entitled *Air Pirate Funnies.*

Disney is the owner of valid copyrights on various works in which appeared characters depicted in a series of cartoon drawings. Defendants, in its magazines, copied the graphic depiction of several of these characters, including Mickey and Minnie Mouse, Donald Duck, The Three Little Pigs and Goofy. The characters in defendants' magazines bore a marked similarity to those of plaintiff. The names of defendants' characters were the same names used in plaintiff's work. However, the themes of defendants' publications differed markedly from those of Disney. While Disney sought only to foster "an image of innocent delightfulness," defendants had used the characters in "an underground comic book which had placed several well-known Disney cartoon characters in incongruous settings where they engaged in activities clearly antithetical to the accepted Mickey Mouse world of scrubbed faces, bright smiles and happy endings." It centered around "a rather bawdy depiction of the Disney characters as active members of a free thinking, promiscuous, drug ingesting counter-culture."

Disney filed a complaint alleging copyright and trademark infringement, unfair competition, trade disparagement and interference with its business. Further, Disney sought injunctive relief, destruction of infringing materials, damages, costs and attorneys fees.

The District Court awarded Disney a temporary restraining order and granted its motion for a preliminary injunction. Three years later, that Court granted Disney's request for a permanent injunction

79

and ordered defendants to deliver all infringing material to Disney's counsel.

On appeal, the Court of Appeals considered only the question of defendants' liability.

The first issue which the Court decided was whether the new Copyright Act or the prior statute controlled. The Court cited the provision of the new Act which specifies that all causes of action which arose under the Copyright Act before January 1, 1978 "shall be governed by Title 17 as it existed when the cause of action arose." To the extent that the legal issues in the case were controlled by statute, the old act governed.

Defendants then argued that characters are never copyrightable and therefore cannot in any way constitute a copyrightable component part. The Court rejected this argument, indicating that it "flies in the face of a series of cases dating back to 1914 that have held comic strip characters protectable under the old Copyright Act." The opinion noted that "it is true that this Court's opinion in *Warner Brothers Pictures v. Columbia Broadcasting System* . . . lends some support to the position that characters ordinarily are not copyrightable. There the mystery writer Dashiell Hammett and his publisher entered into a 1930 contract with Warner Brothers giving the movie production company copyright and various other rights to a 'certain story . . . entitled Maltese Falcon' involving the fictional detective Sam Spade. In 1946, Hammett and other defendants used the Maltese Falcon characters in other writings, causing Warner Brothers to sue for copyright infringement . . ."

In that case, it was held that the character rights with the names were not within the grants and that a restriction on the author's future use of a character was unreasonable, at least when the characters were merely vehicles for the story and did not really constitute the story being told.

The *Walt Disney* opinion made a distinction between literary characters, as in the *Sam Spade* case, and comic book characters. While it is difficult to delineate distinctively a literary character, when the author can add a visual image, the difficulty is reduced. The Court stated: "Put another way, while many literary characters may embody little more than an unprotected idea . . . a comic book character, which has a physical as well as conceptual qualities, is more likely to contain some unique elements of expression. Because comic book characters therefore are distinguishable from literary characters, the Warner Brothers language does not preclude protection of Disney's characters."[2]

The defendants also claimed that the infringement should be excused as permissible fair use because the copying was done to parody Disney's cartoons.

The Court admitted that the establishment of standards for applying fair use as a defense in parody and other cases has been a source of considerable attention and dispute. "As a general matter, while some commentators have urged that the fair use defense depends only on whether the infringing work fills the demand for the original . . . this Court and others have also consistently focused on the substantiality of the taking."

It then cited two cases, one eliminating from the fair use defense near-verbatim copying and the other analyzing the substantiality of the copying in the context of whether the parodist appropriated a greater amount of the original work than was necessary to "recall or conjure up" the object of his satire.

The opinion indicated that there was no need to decide whether the copying was so substantial as to be virtually verbatim because the defendants here took more than was necessary to recall or conjure up the object of the satire. It stated:

"In evaluating how much of a taking was necessary to recall or conjure up the original, it is first important to recognize that given the widespread public recognition of the major characters involved here, such as Mickey Mouse and Donald Duck . . . in comparison with other characters very little would have been necessary to place Mickey Mouse and his image in the minds of the readers. Second, when the medium involved is a comic book, a recognizable caricature is not difficult to draw, so that an alternative that involves less copying is more likely to be available than if a speech, for instance, is parodied. Also significant is the fact that the essence of this parody did not focus on how the characters looked, but rather parodied their personalities, their wholesomeness and their innocence. Thus, arguably, defendants' copying could have been justified as necessary more easily if they had paralleled closely (with a few significant twists) Disney characters and their actions in a manner that conjured up the particular elements of the innocence of the characters that were to be satirized. While greater license may be necessary under those circumstances, here the copying of the graphic image appears to have no other purpose than to track Disney's work as a whole as closely as possible."

The Court then indicated that a balance must be struck between the need to take as much of a work as is necessary to make the "best parody" and the rights of the copyright owner in his original expression. That balance has been struck by giving the parodist what is necessary to conjure of the original, a standard which was exceeded in this instance. By copying the images in their entirety, defendants took more than was necessary to place firmly in the reader's mind the parodied work and those specific attributes that were to be satirized.

Because the amount of defendants' copying exceeded permissible levels, summary judgment was proper.

FOOTNOTES

1.   Walt Disney Productions v. Air Pirates, 581 F.2d 751 (9th Cir. 1978), *cert. denied*, 439 U.S. 1132 (1979).

2.   The courts are still in conflict on the issue of whether or not literary characters, *per se* are copyrightable. *See Nimmer on Copyright*, Section 2.12 (1982).

"Scarlet Fever"—Parody or Adaptation?

A United States District Court has held that a play entitled "Scarlet Fever" is not a spoof or parody, but rather an infringement upon the interests of certain copyright proprietors in and to the novel and the film "Gone With The Wind."[1]

Plaintiffs in that action were Metro-Goldwyn-Mayer Inc. which owns the copyright for the film "Gone With The Wind," The MacMillan Company, Inc., the holder of the copyright for the novel bearing that name, Stephens Mitchell and Trust Company Bank in their capacity as Trustee for certain heirs of Margaret Mitchell, the owner of certain residual interests, including stage rights, in the aforesaid copyrighted works and derivatives thereof. Defendants were the owners, producers and creators of the musical production entitled "Scarlet Fever" which was to have begun public performances in Atlanta, Georgia on September 21, 1979.

"Scarlet Fever" is a three hour, three act play based primarily on the film "Gone With The Wind." As does the film, it opens with a scene at Tara and moves in sequence through the major episodes of that film, in condensed form and omitting certain scenes, and ends as Rhett Butler leaves Scarlet O'Hara. Throughout the various scenes there are interspersed original songs and dance routines.

According to the Court:

"Although modern vernacular has been employed in certain scenes in 'Scarlet Fever,' the script on a scene by scene basis is largely faithful to that of the film. The play also utilizes backdrops depicting scenes reminiscent of the major settings in the film, for example, the plantation house at Tara and the train depot in Atlanta with flames in the background. However, the names of the major characters have been changed so that they are, for example, Shady Charlotte O'Mara, Brett Studler, Melody Hampton, Ansley Mall, and so forth. Further, Shady Charlotte's plantation is dubbed 'Tiara'; Ansley's home, 'Thirteen Elms.'"

After having viewed both "Scarlet Fever" and the film "Gone With The Wind" the Court concluded that "Scarlet Fever" is not entitled to the fair use defense often recognized as a source of protection for certain forms of comment upon copyright works. Taken in its entirety, "Scarlet Fever" is not the sort of original critical comment meant to be protected by the fair use defense, but rather is predominately a derivative or adaptive use of the copyrighted film and novel. Further, to the extent the proposed production of the play contains critical comments in the form of parody or satire, the Court concluded that defendants have drawn upon the copyrighted work far more extensively than is permitted to "conjure up" the subjects or characters parodied.

In discussing the proof by plaintiffs of a *prima facie* case, the Court indicated that one method of proving copying by defendants is to show substantial similarity between the copyrighted and the infringing works. In this regard the "ordinary observation or impression" test may be employed in which there must appear to be substantial similarity to the ordinary observer, so that the alleged copy comes so near to the original as to give the audience the idea created by the original.

In finding a substantial similarity between "Scarlet Fever" and the copyrighted works, the Court noted that the foundation materials of locale, setting, characters, situations and relationships are basically the same in both. The storyline in "Scarlet Fever" is nearly identical to that in the film, although it is somewhat condensed. The dialogue is very often near-verbatim although again condensed and at times inserting modern vernacular; the theme and characterization of the two works also were found to be very similar, although the treatment of these elements is at times more comical in "Scarlet Fever" than in the film "Gone With The Wind."

The defendants basically agreed that "Scarlet Fever" is a comic version of the film and novel "Gone With The Wind" but argued that the nature of the comedy in the play is parody or satire and therefore protected by the fair use defense to copyright infringement.

In addressing this argument and looking at the play as a whole, the Court found that "Scarlet Fever" is neither a parody nor a satire but rather, a musical adaptation of both the film and the novel, generally in the nature of comedy, with some elements of parody but also with elements of tragedy or straight drama.

The Court accepted the following definitions of parody and satire which were put forth by the defendants:

"A parody is a work in which the language or style of another work is closely imitated or mimicked for comic effect or ridicule. A satire is a work which holds up the vices or shortcomings of an individual or institution to ridicule or derision, usually with an intent to stimulate change; the use of wit, irony or sarcasm for the purpose of exposing and discrediting vice or folly."

It added to the definition the caveat that in order to constitute the type of parody eligible for fair use protection, parody must do more than merely achieve comic effect. It must also make some critical comment or statement about the original work which reflects the original perspective of the parodist—thereby giving the parody social value beyond its entertainment function.

Applying this view to "Scarlet Fever," the Court concluded that the play is not a parody because the work as a whole is not a critical commentary on either the film or the novel "Gone With The Wind." The inconsistent use of parody and satire in "Scarlet Fever" deprives the play of the overall effect or impression of parody or satire. Several examples were cited by the Court in support of its conclusion.

Even if "Scarlet Fever" were a parody or satire in its overall effect, the Court found that the play still is not protected by fair use because it incorporates more material from the film and novel than fair use allows. Four guidelines enumerated by 17 U.S.C. Section 107 of the Coypright Act were cited by the Court to aid in determining whether fair use applies:

"(1)   the purpose and character of the use, including whether such use is of a commercial nature or is for nonprofit educational purposes;

"(2)   the nature of the copyrighted work;

"(3)   the amount and substantiality of the portion used in relation to the copyrighted works as a whole; and

"(4)   the effect of the use upon the potential market for or value of the copyrighted work."

Addressing the third such factor, the Court cited the so-called "Benny"[2] test which holds that the exact or near-verbatim copying of a copyrighted work prevents the application of a fair use defense, even if the infringing work is a parody or satire. "The fact that a serious dramatic work is copied practically verbatim, and then presented with actors walking on their hands or with other grotes-queries, does not avoid infringement of the copyright."

Although there is a near-verbatim copying by "Scarlet Fever" of the dialogue and other elements of the film "Gone With The Wind," the Court concluded that there was enough originality in "Scarlet Fever," particularly the songs contained therein, to enable it to pass the "Benny" test, although barely.

However, the Court felt that "Scarlet Fever" incorporates much more of "Gone With The Wind" than necessary to "recall or conjure up" the original work, and therefore no fair use applies. This test allows the parodist sufficient latitude to cause his reader or viewer to recall or conjure up the original work, but when the borrowing from the original is to a far greater degree than that required for that purpose, the defense of fair use will be rejected. Because "Scarlet Fever" so closely follows the general plot of the film "Gone With The Wind," copies specific incidents and details extensively and reproduces significant portions of the dialogue in nearly identical manner, the Court felt that the copying was far more extensive than necessary to conjure up or recall the original work.

The Court also concluded that, contrary to the argument of de-fendants, "Scarlet Fever" is likely to harm the potential market for or value of the derivative use of "Gone With The Wind" in the form of a theatrical adaptation.

Noting that a previously authorized stage version of "Gone With The Wind" was a failure, the Court indicated that it would be an unreasonable assumption to conclude that any future production of "Gone With The Wind" would be the same or similar to the past failure. Indeed, in view of the highly positive audience response to the production of "Scarlet Fever" which was viewed by the Court, the Court felt that a future stage production of "Gone With The Wind" superior to the earlier failure was likely to succeed and therefore "Scarlet Fever" could harm a potential market for or value of a stage version of "Gone With The Wind."

The Court acknowledged that such an analysis is speculative, but indicated that speculation is inherent in the nature of a potential market for a future derivative use.

In support of its speculation, the Court cited what Nimmer calls the "fundamental test."[3] That test requires that a comparison be made not merely of the media in which the two works may appear, but rather in terms of the function of each such work regardless of media. If both the plaintiffs and defendants works are used for the same purpose, then under the functional test the defense of fair use should not be available since the defendants' work serves the same function as that of the plaintiffs.

Asserting that the overall function of both the film and the novel "Gone With The Wind" is to entertain, and concluding that "Scarlet Fever" is not a parody or satire and its overall function is not criticism, comment, reporting or teaching, the Court concluded that the overall function of "Scarlet Fever" also is to entertain. Because the function of the two works is identical and similarity of medium is not relevant to application of the functional test, the conclusion reached is that the potential value of the film and novel "Gone With The Wind" will be diminished if the presentation of "Scarlet Fever" is not enjoined.

In summary, the Court stated that "Scarlet Fever" is neither a parody nor a satire with respect to "fair use" protection, and further than even if "Scarlet Fever" were a parody or satire, "Scarlet Fever" would not be protected by "fair use" because it copies more of "Gone With The Wind" than is allowed. Also, "Scarlet Fever" does not warrant "fair use" protection because it has the same function as "Gone With The Wind" under the "functional test" and therefore is likely to harm the potential market for or value of the copyrighted work.

FOOTNOTES

1. Metro-Goldwyn-Mayer, Inc. v. Showcase Atlanta Cooperative Productions, Inc., No. C79-1766A. Copyright L. Rep. ¶ 25, 122, (N. D. Ga. Oct. 12, 1979).

2. *See* Benny v. Loew's, Inc., 239 F.2d 532 (9th Cir. 1956), *aff'd*, Columbia Broadcasting System, Inc. v. Loew's, Inc., 356 U.S. 43 (1958).

3. 3 Nimmer, *The Law of Copyright*, Section 13.05(B).

Wrestling with a Fair Use Defense

The U.S. Court of Appeals for the Second Circuit has upheld the judgment of the District court finding the American Broadcasting Company and ABC Sports, Inc. ("ABC") liable for copyright infringement.

The decision related to a 28-minute film entitled "Champion" which was produced during the 1970-71 college term by two students enrolled at Iowa State University. Financed jointly by Iowa State University Research Foundation ("Iowa") and the family of Dan Gable, the film presented a short biography of Gable, a champion wrestler who ultimately won a Gold Medal at the 1972 Opympic Games. The film contained comments by Gable and his family, coaches and teammates accompanied by scenes of his wrestling matches, training sessions and home life.

James Doran, one of the two students who had produced the picture, was granted by Iowa the right to license the first television broadcast, subject to the consent of the University. All other rights in and to the film were retained by Iowa, which obtained a valid statutory copyright relating thereto. Prior to the summer of 1972, Doran was unsuccessful in his attempt to sell the television rights.

During August of 1972, while Doran was employed by ABC in connection with its telecast of the Olympic Games, he overheard two ABC producers lamenting the fact that ABC's film crews had not provided sufficient background biographical footage of Gable. He informed one of the producers, Don Ohlmeyer, of the existence of "Champion" and thereafter gave him a copy of the film.

Ohlmeyer then made a videotape copy of all or a portion of the picture (it not being established at trial as to how much of the film actually was copied).

According to Ohlmeyer, he told Doran that although he would try to obtain for him compensation of $250, he could not guarantee this payment because of budgetary constraints. Doran's response supposedly was that he was not interested in payment, but would

89

be pleased simply to have his film on television. Doran disputed this version, alleging that Ohlmeyer promised to investigate compensation, but did not offer to purchase the film. As a result, Doran believed that he had not entered into any agreement with ABC and that ABC was never granted any rights to broadcast "Champion."

When Doran saw edited portions of the film on ABC's Olympic telecast, he notified Iowa, and the University thereafter attempted to reach a settlement with ABC. ABC repeatedly denied that any part of "Champion" had been used, but after Iowa filed a suit in 1975 alleging copyright infringement and after discovery was held, ABC admitted three uses of the film: seven to twelve seconds shown on ABC's pre-Olympic telecast on August 25, 1972; two and one-half minutes used as part of an ABC report on Gable before his first Olympic wrestling match on August 27; and eight seconds telecast in connection with Gable's appearance on ABC's Superstars program in February, 1974 after Iowa had first complained in writing to ABC. The trial judge also found that Ohlmeyer's original production of a videotape of at least portions of the film constituted a fourth instance of infringement. (It should be noted that no significant audio portions of "Champion" were used by ABC and that the network edited and rearranged the segments it did broadcast).

Admitting all allegations of copying, ABC contended during a two day trial on the issue of liability that its uses of the film were protected by the defense of fair use. The District Court rejected this defense. Further, noting that Iowa had not been consulted prior to ABC's telecast of portions of "Champion" and therefore was unable to "consent" to the use by ABC as required by the agreement between Iowa and Doran, it found that no agreement ever had been reached between ABC and Doran.

The District Court found that "defendants appropriated something of value for which, from the nature and extent of their business, they were well prepared to pay" rendering their use of "Champion" unfair. After a subsequent trial on damages, the District Court awarded statutory damages of $15,250; $250 for ABC's initial copying of the film and $5,000 for each of the three televised uses. The Court also awarded $17,500 in attorneys' fees. The amount or computation of damages and fees were not challenged by ABC on appeal; rather, ABC urged that the District Court incorrectly rejected its defense of fair use.

In its opinion, the Court of Appeals cited the four factors which have traditionally been consulted in fair use cases: (1) the purpose and character of the use; (2) the nature of the copyrighted work; (3) the amount and substantiality of material used in relation to the copyrighted work as a whole; and (4) the effect of the use on the copyright holder's potential market for the work. (These criteria have been incorporated in Section 107 of the new Copyright Act, which did not govern the instant case because Iowa's copyright was secured prior to the effective date of the Act).

ABC's defense relied heavily on the purpose and character of the use. It argued that the Court should give great weight to the fact that its purpose was to disseminate the biography of an important public figure involved in an event of great public interest and that there is a public benefit in encouraging the development of historical and biographical works suitable for mass distribution.

The Court distinguished between ABC's right to use any factual information revealed in "Champion" as opposed to the manner of Iowa's expression of that information which, as embodied in the portions of the film, were not available for ABC's use. The Court cited the case of the Human Cannonball[1] which held that a television newscast could report the fact of a performance but could not broadcast the entire actual event without compensating the performer. The Court stated that: "The fair use doctrine is not a license for corporate theft, empowering a court to ignore a copyright whenever it determines the underlying work contains materials of possible public importance. Indeed, we do not suppose that appellants would embrace their own defense theory if another litigant sought to apply it to the ABC evening news."

ABC sought to characterize the nature of "Champion" as an educational film with no significant market. The Court rejected this approach, noting that Iowa contemplated television exposure for the film and that the short vignettes used by ABC on the lives of Olympic athletes during the 1972 coverage were essentially of the same genre as "Champion." Citing Professor Nimmer, the Court noted that where the two works in issue fulfill the same function, the scope of fair use is constricted.[2] In regard to the amount and substantiality of the material used, the Court rejected ABC's argument that its use of only 2½ minutes of a 28-minute film was insignificant and concluded that, obviously ABC found the footage essential or it would not have actually broadcast eight percent of the film.

Finally, the Court discussed the defense that there did not appear to be a significant adverse effect on the market for the film as a result of ABC's broadcast. Although the available evidence suggested that the market value of "Champion" increased after ABC's telecast, it was the Court's opinion that a significantly potential market to Iowa was foreclosed—the sale of its film for use on television in connection with Olympics. When ABC telecast the film without purchasing the rights, it usurped an extremely significant market. Iowa had no right to insist that ABC use its film, but its copyright entitled it to attempt to exploit the commercial market controlled by ABC and, if it could not, to withhold permission to use the film in that market.

The Court noted that it took into consideration in arriving at its decision the equitable considerations relating to the case. It could not ignore the fact, found by the District judge, that ABC copied "Champion" while purporting to assess its value for possible purchase or that the network repeatedly denied that it ever had used the film.

FOOTNOTES

1.   Zacchini v. Scripps-Howard Broadcasting Co., 433 U.S. 562 (1977).

2.   *Nimmer on Copyright*, Section 13.05 [B] at 13-38.

Regulations Regarding Copyright Notice

In an effort to offer guidance to those seeking to copyright "visually perceptible works," including books, motion pictures, games, and pictorial, graphic and sculptural works, the Register of Copyrights has promulgated regulations regarding the methods of affixation of the copyright notice for such works.[1] The regulations, initially proposed in 1977, were deemed effective with respect to copies of these works publicly distributed on or after December 1, 1981, and provide guidance by specifying examples of methods of affixation of notice acceptable under copyright law.

The Copyright Act of 1976 prescribes a general requirement of notice of copyright in Section 401(a):

"Whenever a work protected under this title is published in the United States or elsewhere by authority of the copyright owner, a notice of copyright as provided by this section shall be placed on all publicly distributed copies from which the work can be visually perceived, either directly or with the aid of a machine or device."[2]

Although the form of notice is clearly specified in the Copyright Act of 1976,[3] Section 401(c), relating to position of notice, provides only that the notice be affixed to the copies "in such manner and location as to give reasonable notice of the claim of copyright"; this section then empowers the Register of Copyrights to set forth by regulation "as examples, specific methods of affixation and positions of the notice on various types of works that will satisfy this requirement," but provides further that these specifications "shall not be considered exhaustive." The rationale for the approach of Section 401(c) was that the provision would permit flexibility, while the regulations would "offer substantial guidance and avoid a good deal of uncertainty." In addition, as the specifications are not to be considered "exhaustive," a notice "placed or affixed in some other way might also comply with the law if it were found to 'give reasonable notice' of the copyright claim."[4]

Section 401(c) and the Copyright Office's regulations liberalized the provisions of Section 20 of the Copyright Act of 1909, which imposed stringent limits on the acceptable position of notice for certain works, and only vague requirements with respect to other works. Under the old law, for example, notice for books was required to be affixed on the "title page or the page immediately following," notice for periodicals was to be affixed "either upon the title page or the first page of text of each separate number or under the title heading," and notice for a musical work was to be applied "either upon its title page or the first page of music."[5] Case law, and not the Copyright Act of 1909, dictated appropriate notice positions with respect to contributions to collective works, motion pictures, and other audiovisual works. The confusion engendered by the notice requirements of the old law[6] hopefully will be alleviated by the flexible approach of Section 401(c).

The basic concept of the regulations promulgated by the Register of Copyrights appears in paragraph (c), dealing with the manner of affixation and position generally, which states that ". . . the acceptability of a notice depends upon its being permanently legible to an ordinary user of the work under normal conditions of use, and affixed to the copies in such manner and position that, when affixed, it is not concealed from view upon reasonable examination." This general provision specifies further that where notice is not affixed in one of the precise locations prescribed by the regulations, "but a person looking in one of those locations would be reasonably certain to find a notice in another somewhat different location," then that notice is deemed acceptable.

This provision strikes a balance not achieved in the 1909 Act and appears to accomplish the goals set forth in the House Report commentary respecting Section 401 of the 1976 Act.[7] The regulations induce the use of notice and thus preserve the values of the notice requirement—informing the public as to whether a particular work is copyrighted and preventing innocent persons from subjecting themselves to penalties imposed upon infringers of copyright, identifying the copyright owner, showing the date of publication and placing in the public domain published material that no one is interested in copyrighting. At the same time, the regulations attempt to avoid the arbitrary forfeiture of copyright protection which, under the 1909 Act, might have resulted from an unintentional or relatively minor error in the placement of notice.

Having outlined this basic framework, the regulations delineate specific examples of methods of affixation and positions of the copyright notice which will be considered "acceptable" under the Copyright Act of 1976 for various types of works. Prior to delineating these specific examples, the regulations provide a detailed list of definitions of terms used in the examples, including definitions of "page," "leaf," "book form," "title page," "front page" and "back page," "masthead," and "single-leaf work," as well as distinctions among these terms, thus tending to obviate such problems as determining what, precisely, constitutes a "title page," the subject of controversy in several cases.[8]

The first category of examples relates to affixation of notice in connection with "works published in book form."[9] With respect to these works, the position of notice of copyright will be acceptable if it is reproduced in any of a number of locations, including the title page or the page immediately following the title page; either side of the front or back cover; the first or the last page of the main body of the work; or any page between the front page and the first page of the main body of the work, if there are not more than ten pages between the front page and the first page and if the notice is prominent and separate from other matter on the page where it appears. In addition, with respect to works published as an issue of a periodical or serial, notice is also acceptable if located as a part of or adjacent to the masthead, on the same page as the masthead if the notice is prominent, or adjacent to a prominent heading containing the title of the periodical or the serial at or near the front of the issue. With respect to musical works, in addition to the aforementioned locations, notice on the first page of music is deemed acceptable.

The second major category of examples specifies notice positions for contributions to collective works, a category not specifically included in the notice provisions of the 1909 Act. The Copyright Act of 1976 specifies in Section 404 that a separate contribution to a collective work "may bear its own notice of copyright, as provided in Sections 401 through 403," although a single notice for the collective work is sufficient to satisfy the notice requirement for the separate contributions it contains.

With respect to separate contributions of less than one page in length, notice may be under the title, adjacent to the contribution, or on the same page as the contribution, if the notice clearly applies to the contribution. Notice for contributions in excess of one page in length may be affixed in any of a number of specified locations, including the first page of the main body of the contribution, and following the end of the contribution. The regulation even permits the placement of notice "in a clearly identified and readily accessible table of contents or listing of acknowledgments appearing near the front or back of the collective work as a whole."[10]

Examples also are included of acceptable notice locations for two additional classes of work not specifically covered by the notice provisions of the 1909 Act—works reproduced in machine-readable copies, such as filmstrips, slide films and microform, and motion pictures and other audiovisual works.[11] With respect to audiovisual works, the affixation of copyright notice is acceptable if it is "embodied in the copies by a photomechanical, or electronic process, in such a position that it would ordinarily appear whenever the work is performed in its entirety," and if it is located with or near the title, with the credits, or at the beginning or end of the work. For audiovisual works of 60 seconds or less in duration, notice is only required to be on the leader of the film or tape apparent to the projectionist or broadcaster, although the other locations specified for audiovisual works also would be acceptable.

In response to emerging areas of new technology, the regulations provide specifically for acceptable positions of notice for works reproduced in machine-readable copies, such as "magnetic tapes or discs, punched cards or the like, from which the work cannot ordinarily be perceived except with the aid of a machine." Notice for this class of works may be affixed so that, with respect to printouts of the work, it appears near the title or at the end of the work, or so that it appears at "the user's terminal at sign on" or is continuously on terminal display, or so that it appears on a label securely affixed to the permanent receptacle for the works. In a similar effort to provide for potential problems before they arise, and in response to the surge in sales of videocassettes and similar devices to the public for private use, the regulations indicate that, in the case of "a motion picture or other audiovisual work that is distributed to the public for private use, the notice may be affixed . . . on the housing or container, if it is a permanent receptable for the work."

Finally, the provisions of the regulations relating to pictorial, graphic and sculptural works are intended to rectify a wide variety of controversy engendered with respect to the proper position of notice for commercial designs, jewelry, toys, games, and textiles.[12] In regard to these categories of works, problems arose frequently under the 1909 Act with respect to the appropriate locations for copyright notice in the case of repetitive designs in textiles, wallpaper, and wrapping paper, and in the case of works containing copyright notice on their selvage, material often discarded in the use of the works, such as the manufacture of clothing.

In response to these problems, the Register of Copyrights promulgated the regulation that, where a work "is reproduced in copies consisting of sheet-like or strip material bearing multiple or continuous reproductions of the work, the notice may be applied: (i) to the reproduction itself; (ii) to the margin, selvage, or reverse side of the material at frequent and regular intervals; or (iii) if the material contains neither a selvage nor a reverse side, to tags or labels, attached to the copies . . . or containers housing them in such a way that a notice is visible while the copies are passing through their normal channels of commerce."[13]

With respect to other pictorial, graphic and sculptural works, notice for two-dimensional works must be "durably" affixed, directly or by label, to the front or back of the copies, or to other material to which the copies are "durably attached" or in which they are permanently housed; notice for three-dimensional copies is similar, except that it must be attached to a "visible" portion of the work. The regulation for pictorial, graphic and sculptural works provides further that, if the work is "permanently housed in a container, such as a game or puzzle, a notice reproduced on the permanent container is acceptable."

Through these regulations, the Register of Copyrights has attempted both to resolve controversies which arose under the notice affixation provisions (or lack thereof) under the 1909 Act, and to address problems which conceivably could arise under the 1976 Act by virtue of rapidly developing new technology and expanding views of copyrightable subject matter. In addition, through the flexible approach of these regulations requiring notice to be visible upon "reasonable" examination of the work, the Register of Copyrights has attemped to achieve a fair balance between encouraging the affixation of copyright notice to publicly distributed works and avoiding the harsh result of forfeiture of copyright through a misplaced notice.

FOOTNOTES

1.   37 C.F.R. Section 201.20 (1981).
2.   17 U.S.C. Section 401(a) (1976).
3.   17 U.S.C. Section 401(b) (1976).
4.   H.R. Rep. No. 94-1476, 94th Cong., 2d Sess. (1976) ("House Report") 144.
5.   17. U.S.C. Section 20 (1909).
6.   *Cf.* A Latman, *The Copyright Law*, at 133-37 (1979).
7.   House Report at 143.
8.   *See* Powell v. Stransky, 98 F. Supp. 434 (S.Dakota 1951).
9.   37 C.F.R. Section 201.20(d) (1981).
10.   37 C.F.R. Section 201.20(f)(ii) (1981).
11.   37 C.F.R. Section 201.20(g), (h) (1981).
12.   Peter Pan Fabrics, Inc. v. Martin Weiner Corp., 274 F.2d 487 (2d Cir. 1960).
13.   37 C.F.R. Section 201.20(i)(4) (1981).

Chapter Four

Representation—Managers, Agents, Attorneys

The Personal Manager

The demise of the system under which motion picture stars were signed to long-term agreements with motion picture companies, the advent of television as a significant market for a performer's talents and the rise in popularity of rock and roll all contributed to the ascendancy of the personal manager in the 1950s as a force in the entertainment industry. Today, many personal managers wield significant power as a result of their relationship with, and in some cases control over, the talent which they represent. Indeed, a few managers, capitalizing on their abilities and the success of their clients, have become successful motion picture producers, presenters of spectacular live performances and entrepreneurs in other areas of entertainment not strictly relating to management activities.

The following statement by a then prominent record executive is illustrative of the perception of many in the entertainment industry regarding the role and the importance of personal management:

"In the late 1950's, the nature of the music changed and the nature of the recording artists changed and since that time, the great preponderance of the music business is represented by very young, very unsophisticated, very immature and not always quite sane recording artists. The nature of our relationship with them is now so intricate . . .

"The criteria we base our selection of talent on is, A, of course, the talent, the ability to write, or sing songs or play instruments. And secondly, the strength and the involvement of strong personal management . . .

"The personal manager adds so many colors to the career of an artist as opposed to the agency which has an important role, but a very one-dimensional role, and that's securing employment, but employment is only one part of the career . . .

"Personal managers to us in addition to serving as our conscience and our guide in the packaging and merchandising, the exploitation, the production of records, and then coordinating the exploitation after the record is out with working with the agency on the other

101

side to send the artist on a personal appearance tour concurrent with the release of our record; all these subtleties in development artists are absolutely vital and we would not—we would be very hesitant to sign an artist to our label who did not have good personal manager representation. The agency can come later, that's an added attraction later on and a choice of agencies . . . all of whom can deliver the same function.

"The personal manager babysits. You have a number of groups, five and six young people who have great conflicts within themselves. Keeping these groups together on the road, the stress and constant pressure of press and radio and fans and playing night after night at the ball parks and forums and Madison Square Gardens. It would appear to me that the role of personal manager . . . is absolutely vital to the career of the great bulk of recording artists today . . . I know that from our standpoint, the presence of the management as a prod to us and as a liaison with the talent is vital, and there have been some legendary . . . personal manager-artists' stories in our record business . . . and there is no agency that I have ever had experience with that have handled their careers with the same degree of care, the same degree of specific colorings or presentation and flair for showmanship as a personal manager . . ."[1]

A proposed form of agreement between manager and artist promulgated by the Conference of Personal Managers sets forth in the second paragraph several functions which the manager ("you") is to perform for the artist ("me") as and when requested by the artist. They are listed and discussed here in the order presented in that contract.

a) "Advise and counsel in the selection of literary, artistic and musical material." This provision focuses on the creative endeavors of the manager. In the case of a musical performer, the selection of the compositions to be recorded and the preparation of a musical act are extremely important. Similarly, the career of an actor or actress may rise and fall on the nature of the dramatic properties and the roles which he or she selects.

b) "Advise and counsel in any and all matters pertaining to publicity, public relations and advertising." In this clause, the thrust is the image which the artist projects to the industry and to consumers. The manager may be called upon to select and deal with public relations firms, to cause to be created and disseminated appropriate photographs, biographical and similar material and to make certain that all advertising relating to the artist is consistent with the image sought to be projected and the role or performance which is being rendered.

c) "Advise and counsel with relation to the adoption of proper format for the presentation of my artistic talents and in the determination of proper style, mood, setting, business and characterization in keeping with my talents." This clause also relates to the creative functions of the manager and is tied closely with the activities of the manager referred to in section (a) above.

d) "Advise, counsel and direct in the selection of artistic talent to assist, accompany or embellish my artistic presentation." In the activities of a musical performer, the arranger, producer, back-up singers, musicians and musical director all are integral components of the sound and feeling which is created. In the case of an actor or actress, the director, producer, cinematographer, choreographer, writer and other similar elements all must be woven together to make the project a success.

e) "Advise and counsel with regard to general practices in the entertainment and amusement industries and with respect to such matters of which you may have knowledge concerning compensation and privileges extended for similar artistic values." Here the reference is to the manager as negotiator and businessman. Given the present entertainment client, a manager who wishes to represent his client properly must have a knowledge, not only of one particular industry such as music, but of the entertainment industry as a whole. For example, if a manager were representing a performer in a motion picture who, because of his box office appeal, was also the production entity for the picture, negotiations would be required in several of the following areas: a property would be acquired and "packaged" by causing a screenplay to be written and possibly a director or other star to be engaged; an arrangement for domestic distribution of the picture would be concluded and would involve some financing arrangements; perhaps pre-sales of the picture would be made to network television, syndicated television, and pay television; agreements might be entered into with foreign distributors for the picture in an effort to obtain additional financing for same; in connection with the foregoing, negotiations with a lending institute might be conducted in order to use the agreements as collateral for the fifor the financing of the picture; agreements involving cassette and videodisc rights might be concluded; the music contained in the picture might be suitable for an arrangement with a record company to distribute a soundtrack album; the screenplay for the picture might serve as the basis for an agreement with a publisher to distribute a novelization; other elements in the picture might be the subject of merchandising activities. All of the foregoing would require the advice and counsel of the manager together with the attorney, accountant and other business advisors of the client.

f) "Advise and counsel concerning the selection of theatrical agencies, artists' managers, and persons, firms and corporations who will counsel, advise, seek and procure employment and engagements for me." In New York and in California there are statutes which restrict the manager from engaging in activities which amount to "seeking employment." Accordingly, the manager will work with the artist to obtain the services of a suitable agent who will be the entity which attempts to procure employment. Further, the manager will work with attorneys, business managers, accountants and other third parties involved in the career of the artist. His function in this regard will be as a liaison between the artist and those who must deal with him on a business and professional basis.

The Conference of Personal Managers' form of agreement specifies activities which the manager may perform, but does not begin to describe the extremely close personal relationship that often exists between the artist and manager. It is the intangible aspect of this relationship that is so hard to describe, yet so important in the development of the artist's career. Whether the manager performs his role in the capacity of a dominant father figure, supporting confidant or on another basis, there is little doubt that today employers of performers look upon management as an extremely important ingredient in the total entertainment package.

FOOTNOTES

1.   The Licensing and Regulation of Artists Managers, Personal Managers, and Musicians Bookings Agencies Before The Cal. Senate Comm. on Industrial Relations 60 (Nov. 20, 1975) (statement of

Joe Smith), *cited in* Johnson, N. and Lang, D., "The Personal Manager in the California Entertainment Industry," 52 *So. Cal. L. Rev.* 375,380 (1979).

Summary of Speech for American Bar Association Forum Committee on Entertainment and Sports Industries, September 27, 1980

The *Iman* Case: Model Representation

Managers and agents should note carefully the New York Appellate Court decision in Wilhelmina Model, Inc. ("Wilhelmina") v. Iman Abdulmajid ("Iman").[1] In that case, Wilhelmina, a model's representative, was denied its attempt to prevent Iman, a prominent model, from changing her representation.

In 1975, Iman was discovered in her native country of Kenya by Peter Beard, a professional photographer. After her picture had been sent to Wilhelmina, Iman was urged by the president of that company to come to the United States to pursue a career as a model.

Iman, who was 20 when she arrived in New York, claimed she then spoke English only haltingly, whereas Wilhelmina described her on arrival in the United States as a woman educated at the Nairobi school who spoke impeccable English and four other languages. It is undisputed, however, that shortly after her arrival, Iman signed a contract designating Wilhelmina for a three year period as her sole and exclusive personal and business manager and advisor throughout the world in the fields of modeling, acting, performing and related actitivites. Iman later claimed that she signed the document because she thought it was necessary to do so in order to obtain immigration papers to work in the United States.

The contract contained the following language, similar to that contained in most contracts between performers and their managers and agents:

> I (Iman) acknowledge that my services are extraordinary and unique and there is no adequate remedy at law for a breach of this agreement by me and that in the event of such a breach or attempted breach or threatened breach, you shall be entitled to equitable relief by way of injunction or otherwise.

Such a clause is an attempt to establish the basis for obtaining injunctive relief in the event that the performer decides to engage a new representative. The theory of the manager is that were the performer to switch representatives, the damage done to the original

107

manager would be irreparable and not compensable by money alone. Factors such as the harm to the reputation of the manager in the entertainment community, the unique abilities of the original manager vis-à-vis others as well as the loss of the special and unique talents of the performer which would be impossible to replace all would be relevant in the decision of a court to grant or deny injunctive relief.

After joining Wilhelmina, Iman became a celebrated model, and her earnings, which in her second year were more than twice those in her first, reflected her success. Thus, when Iman advised Wilhelmina in December of 1977 that she was going to change representatives, Wilhelmina responded by seeking an order to prevent Iman from engaging any company other than Wilhelmina to act as her manager.

The lower court which heard the motion issued an injunction. On appeal, the decision was reversed and the injunction denied.

The Appellate Court concluded that Wilhelmina had not shown that it would suffer irreparable damage as a result of Iman's leaving.

Also it reasoned that because Wilhelmina required all models to sign form contracts containing essentially the same language, Wilhelmina could not argue that it felt Iman's services were truly unique.

Further, to the extent Iman's services were unique, they were unique to the photographers and commercial organizations which hired her, but not to Wilhelmina.

Finally, the Court indicated that it was Iman who had hired and paid Wilhelmina, not vice-versa, and thus money damages awarded to Wilhelmina for breach of contract would be a sufficient remedy.

As a result of this decision, managers representing performers should review and possibly revise the form contracts which they require their clients to sign.

FOOTNOTES

1. Wilhelmina Models, Inc. v. Iman Abdulmajid, 67 App. Div.2d 853, 413 N.Y.2d 21 (1st Dept. 1979).

Variety, July 25, 1979

Supreme Court Explores Equity Franchise System

In its review of the Second Circuit decision in *H.A. Artists & Associates v. Actors' Equity Association,*[1] the Supreme Court held that performing artists' unions have the right to license agents, but may not have the right to impose franchise fees on the agents as part of the regulatory scheme. In its decision, the Court sought to balance the divergent goals of the antitrust laws and the federal labor laws, taking into account their impact on certain unique characteristics of the entertainment industry. In an opinion delivered by Justice Stewart, the Court affirmed in part and reversed in part the Second Circuit's judgment with respect to the legitimacy under the antitrust laws of Actors' Equity's franchising system for the regulation of independent theatrical agents.[2]

The Court affirmed that portion of the Second Circuit opinion which held that the Equity licensing system, and its concomitant regulation of agents, are permissible under the statutory labor exemption of the antitrust laws, in that these regulations are "clearly designed to promote the union's legitimate self-interest."[3] However, the Court did not find, as did the Second Circuit, that franchise fees exacted of Equity's licensed agents as part of the regulatory scheme had been adequately justified by Equity, which proposed a vague correlation between the fees and the cost of implementing the regulatory system. The Court found that these fees could be viewed as subsidizing the regulatory system, but that no adequate relationship between the franchise fees and Equity's legitimate interests exists to justify the imposition of the franchise fees on independent agents.[4]

The disputed franchising system of Actors' Equity, the national union which currently represents approximately 23,000 actors, was established in 1928, a time of high unemployment rates in the theater, to combat the vulnerability of theatrical performers to abuses by agents. These agents could offer the tantalizing possibility of employment, and extract high commissions from their clients, thus

109

undermining collectively bargained rates of compensation between Equity and theatrical producers. Equity's answer to abusive agent practices consisted of a regulatory franchising system for agents, whereby Equity licensed agents who had agreed to certain prescribed conditions of representation, and Equity members were permitted to deal only with agents thus franchised.

The prescribed conditions of this licensing system, at issue before the Supreme Court, included the licensed agent's renunciation of any commission on employment by the client at "scale" or minimum wages, including rehearsal or "chorus" employment, and of any commission on out-of-town expense money. In addition, commissions are limited within ten percent of scale, on the theory that commissions do not necessarily correlate exactly with efforts exerted by the agent who may function only as a producer's "order taker." As a further condition, the one rejected by the Supreme Court, the system requires payment to Equity of a franchise fee of $200 for the initial franchise, $60 a year thereafter per agent, and $40 a year per subagent, which monies are deposited in Equity's general treasury, not segregated from other union funds.

Petitioners, independent theatrical agents who refused to abide by Equity's licensing procedures, challenged the system of regulation as violative of Sections 1 and 2 of the Sherman Act, claiming it constituted price-fixing, an agreement not to compete, a group boycott of unlicensed agents, and monopolization. Both the District Court[5] and the Second Circuit[6] found Equity's actions protected from the reach of the antitrust laws by the statutory labor exemption to these laws, and dismissed petitioners' complaint.

The statutory labor exemption, which serves to shield labor groups from antitrust liability, applies to an organized labor group which has acted in its self-interest, in the absence of any combination with a "non-labor group" or persons not "parties to a labor dispute," in an area properly the subject of union concern. The Second Circuit unanimously affirmed the District Court, finding the agents comprise a labor group because of their substantial "economic interrelationships" with Equity, such that wage competition among members, a legitimate object of union concern could not be controlled without regulation of the agents' fees.[7]

The Supreme Court, in reviewing the decision of the Court of Appeals, recognized the "inherent tension between national antitrust policy, which seeks to maximize competition, and national labor policy, which encourages cooperation among workers to improve the conditions of employment."[8] In reaction to this tension, the Court noted, Congress acted, first in the Clayton Act, and later in the Norris-LaGuardia Act, "to immunize labor unions and labor disputes from challenge under the Sherman Act," and the statutory labor exemptions thus born have been "interpreted broadly as a statement of congressional policy that the courts must not use the antitrust laws as a vehicle to interfere in labor disputes."[9] Citing *Connell Construction Co. v. Plumbers & Steamfitters*,[10] the Court highlighted the balance which must be struck between the goals of federal labor law and antitrust law, stating that union success in organizing members to eliminate competition over wages and working conditions "requires tolerance for the lessening of business competition based on differences in wages and working conditions."[11] The statutory labor exemption is forfeited, however, when a union combines with a "non-labor group" in restraint of trade.

The Court thus found that the District Court had correctly recognized the threshold issue as one of determining whether Equity's franchising system involved any combination between Equity and a non-labor group. In affirming the Second Circuit's holding that agents must be considered a "labor group," and that their controversy with Equity constituted a "labor dispute" within the definition of the Norris-LaGuardia Act, the Court noted certain unique aspects of the entertainment industry. The agent, as middleman between union members and producers is, in the absence of regulation, in a "powerful position to evade the union's negotiated wage structure." The Court found that the "peculiar structure of the legitimate theatre industry, where work is intermittent, where it is customary if not essential for union members to secure employment through agents, and where agents' fees are calculated as a percentage of a member's wage, makes it impossible for the union to defend even the integrity of the minimum wages it has negotiated without regulation of agency fees."[12] Likening the agents' function, that of placing union members in the work force, to the hiring hall functions performed by non-entertainment unions, the Court viewed the franchise system as Equity's "substitute for maintaining a hiring hall," and found the franchise regulations "clearly designed to promote the union's legitimate self-interest."[13]

The Court reversed the Second Circuit with respect to the franchise fee requirement, which had been approved in its extant form as "reasonably related" to the operation of the franchise system. Equity sought to justify the fee as "somehow related to the basic purposes"—the elimination of wage competition, upholding the union wage scale, and the promotion of fair access to jobs—of the Equity regulations. The Supreme Court found the justification inadequate: "[E]ven assuming that the fees no more than cover the costs of administering the regulatory system, this is simply another way of saying that without the fees, the union's regulatory efforts would not be subsidized—and that the dues of Equity's members would perhaps have to be increased to offset the loss of a general revenue source. If Equity did not impose these franchise fees upon the agents, there is no reason to believe that any of its legitimate interests would be affected."[14]

Equity's attempt to analogize the payment of a franchise fee by the agents to the imposition of hiring hall fees on employers in the non-entertainment fields was distinguished on the grounds that, in the hiring hall situation, the fees are borne by the parties benefitting directly from the employment services; the agents, the Court opined, are not such direct beneficiaries.

Justices Brennan and Marshall dissented with respect to the franchise fee issue, finding that the "agents also benefit from the franchising system, which provides an orderly and protective mechanism for pairing actors who seek jobs with producers who seek actors."[15]

Following this decision Equity reached a settlement in which it agreed to discontinue its practice of charging franchise fees. Thereafter Screen Actors Guild, in connection with a suit brought by Talent Representatives Inc., also agreed to discontinue the requirement of franchise fees and to return such fees paid during the two years prior to that settlement.

FOOTNOTES

1. H.A. Artists & Associates v. Actors' Equity Association, 622 F.2d 647 (2d Cir. 1980).

2. H.A. Artists & Associates v. Actors' Equity Association, No. 80-348, U.S.S.Ct., May 26, 1981.

3. *Id.* at 17.
4. *Id.* at 17.
5. 478 F. Supp. 496 (S.D.N.Y. 1979).
6. 622 F.2d 647 (2d Cir. 1980).
7. 622 F.2d at 650, 651.
8. No. 80-348 at 8.
9. *Id.*
10. 421 U.S. 616.
11. No. 80-348.
12. *Id.*
13. *Id.*
14. *Id.*, Brennan, J. and Marshall, J., dissenting.
15. *Id.*

The Entertainment Attorney

An article entitled "Backstage With The Show Business Lawyers" which appeared in an issue of *Juris Doctor Magazine* was accompanied by a picture of a man attired in a tennis outfit, holding racquet in one hand and telephone in the other, presumably conducting his law practice from the tennis court. Although a few entertainment attorneys may practice in this setting, many others practice in a more traditional environment.

There is no stereotype of an entertainment attorney, nor is there a body of requirements which he must fulfill to be classified as such. (The male gender is used herein strictly for convenience; several prominent entertainment attorneys are women). States which certify attorneys as specialists (including California) do not yet award certificates of legal specialization to the entertainment attorney.

Entertainment law, the basis of the entertainment attorney's practice, is an amorphous concept. Endeavors which provide entertainment are not necessarily included in the subject matter of entertainment law. The counsel whose sole client is a gambling casino or an amusement park is not generally considered an entertainment attorney, although one whose sole client is the performing group which appears there is. Arm wrestling matches, though sometimes entertaining, may not enter the province of the entertainment attorney until they are broadcast during halftime of a professional basketball game.

Whether or not an individual is considered an entertainment attorney depends greatly upon the purpose for which the characterization is made, the nature of the matters he handles and his overall clientele.

The practice of the entertainment attorney may focus on matters involving motion pictures, television, home video, theater, music (including record production, publishing and live engagements) and licensing. Performers, writers, directors, producers, distributors, agents and managers are his clientele. His practice may extend to

115

representing clients in the arts—ballet, opera, serious music—and to clients involved in sports, literary publishing, fashion and design.

Entertainment attorneys sometimes specialize in only one of the foregoing areas. A common specialist is the music attorney who represents a combination of performers, producers, record companies and publishers. Typically, he is an adroit negotiator with contacts at companies throughout the industry. Many such attorneys, after becoming involved in the business and artistic aspects of their clients' careers, have left the practice of law to become personal managers or producers.

Motion picture specialists, also active negotiators, often will be, or have as associates, skilled draftsmen; for the typical motion picture project will involve numerous lengthy agreements. Certain of these practitioners who represent prominent motion picture clients have become powerful figures in the industry by virtue of their ability to provide several of such clients as a "package" to be included in a picture. Because multi-million dollar production budgets are common, the aggregate compensation paid to these clients often is substantial.

The vast majority of entertainment attorneys practice in New York or Los Angeles, and several firms have a main office in one and a branch in the other. Although motion picture and television production is concentrated in California, there is much activity in these fields in New York, which also remains as a center of legitimate theater, music activity and literary publishing. Other cities, including Nashville, Memphis, Atlanta and Chicago have developed as sites for production or as headquarters for entertainment companies, with a resultant increase in the number of entertainment lawyers in each city.

The practice of the entertainment attorney has become global in scope. Some motion pictures are wholly or partially financed by foreign tax investments or advances from distributors which will exploit the picture in specified foreign territories. In the music industry, significant sales of records occur abroad, popular performers undertake foreign tours and publishers exploit compositions throughout the world. Licensing on a world-wide basis of television programs produced in the United States also generates substantial revenues.

As international entertainment transactions have proliferated, the body of law affecting entertainment attorneys has expanded. At its core are copyright law and contract law, the former because copyright is the major component of transactions involving creative works, the latter because negotiating, drafting and interpreting contracts consume much of the practitioner's time.

Surrounding this core are those areas of law applicable to each specific matter which the attorney handles. A client raising financing for motion picture or theatrical productions will be affected by securities laws. Tax considerations underlie most transactions of both the corporate and individual client, especially in a field in which the individual's earnings tend to be high. Immigration problems arise in connection with the representation or intended employment of foreign talent. Antitrust questions are presented in the distribution of phonograph records. Labor laws are applicable to talent unions. Frequently the entertainment attorney will engage experts to work with him on these specific matters.

There now exists a wide variety of books, periodicals, law journals, law school courses and seminars relating to the subject of entertainment law. In addition, trade publications such as *Variety* must be read by the entertainment attorney, for often he will render business as well as legal advice and must keep current with industry trends and developments.

The intangible attribute on which the success of an entertainment attorney invariably rests in an ability to understand and deal with the "artistic temperament" so often possessed by his clients. The *Juris Doctor* article cited above states: "But there is one nonnegotiable talent that this lawyer should have. It is a gift that transcends legal wizardry or a good recall of the latest box office tables in *Variety*. This involves a therapist's understanding and a snake-oil salesman's finesse around that mercurial blend of ego and vulnerability known as the 'artistic temperament.'"

Like obscenity, this temperament is easier to recognize than to define. It is characterized by inevitable insecurities fostered by a career in which the artist's performances are constantly evaluated by the public and in which success is often short-lived. It is surrounded by enormous talent and creativity. The product varies from client to client and the attorney-client relationship also varies, with the role of the attorney shifting constantly among that of counselor, sounding board, critic, father and friend.

Rewards of the entertainment attorney include the handling of fascinating subjects which often come to life in productions or performances and the fulfillment of contributing to endeavors which bring pleasure to masses of people.

Chapter Five
Plays and Pictures

Differing Rights of the Screenwriter and the Playwright

The rights which the author of a screenplay transfers to the motion picture producer are fundamentally different from the rights which the author of the "book" for a legitimate stage production licenses to the producer of the play.

For the purposes of this article it will be assumed that the agreement governing the disposition of motion picture rights in and to the screenplay will be in a form similar to that customarily used by many motion picture studios when they acquire rights to a completed original screenplay and that the agreement relating to the disposition of rights in and to the book will be in a form similar to that of the Dramatists Guild Minimum Basic Production Contract. It will also be assumed that the screenwriter is entitled to a percentage of the profits of the motion picture.

The purchaser of rights to a screenplay generally will acquire exclusively and forever all rights to make and perform motion pictures, whether silent, sound, or musical, and to utilize and exploit the picture in theaters and on television. Also acquired will be the right to produce remakes and sequels (the former being the right to make subsequent versions based upon the same property, generally for the purpose of updating the picture; the latter being the right to make subsequent pictures, generally continuing rather than retelling the original story, using identifying factors from the first, but with different plots, sequences, situations and incidents). The producer also will try to obtain the right to cause a television series to be produced based upon the motion picture.

The screenwriter will grant the rights to adapt, modify and translate the screenplay and he will be required to waive any rights of "droit moral" which he has in the property. This waiver is to protect the producer from a claim that the writer has been damaged as a result of the mutilation or other treatment of the work which is not satisfactory to the writer.

121

Specific rights, such as the right to present the work dramatically on the stage with live actors and the right to produce live television broadcasts based upon the work, may be reserved to the author. To protect the investment which he is making in the production of the motion picture, the producer inevitably will require that there be a holdback period during which such reserved rights may not be exploited.

The implied premise of such acquisition agreements is that the writer is one cog, albeit an important one, in the multifaceted affair of producing a picture; an affair in which the producer assembles several entities who individually and collectively have a hand in shaping the screenplay to a workable form, assuming it is used at all, in connection with the picture.

The Minimum Basic Production Contract governing legitimate theater transactions is totally different in concept. Essentially, it is a license to the producer to present a play on the speaking stage in the United States and Canada. The stated premise of this contract is that if the producer successfully does this in a first-class manner, he makes a contribution to the value of the play for other uses. Accordingly, if the producer presents the play for 21 consecutive performances in New York or 64 consecutive performances in or out of New York or one performance in New York if the producer has made a specified prior payment to the author, the producer will acquire rights in addition to the license referred to above. These include the right to receive a percentage of the receipts derived by the author from the disposition of motion picture rights throughout the world and the following rights in the United States and Canada: radio, television, second-class touring, foreign language performances, condensed and tabloid verisons, concert tour versions, commercial uses and play albums. Such additional rights also may include the exclusive right to present the play in the British Isles and the right to reopen the play within a certain period of time after the initial first-class run of the play.

Depending upon how long after the last perfomance of the play these rights are disposed of, the producer will receive from 40 percent of such receipts (for earlier dispositions) to 20 percent thereof (for later ones).

The obvious distinction between the treatment of the above rights relating to the book and the corresponding rights relating to the screenplay is that the author retains the rights to dispose of the former and the purchasing producer ordinarily acquires the rights to dispose of the latter. A related fact is that the producing entity will be the copyright proprietor of the motion picture but not of the play.

Such distinctions between the positions of the respective two authors extend to the creative controls over the ultimate production. The motion picture producer acquires all rights necessary to alter or change the screenplay in any manner which he feels is appropriate and, as previously noted, requires the writer to waive rights of "droit moral." Except in rare instances, he will be authorized to produce the picture using any directorial, acting and other talent which he determines. Conversely, the producer of a play generally acknowledges that the play is an artistic creation of the author and agrees that the author is entitled to approval over the cast and director, and when appropriate, conductor and dance director. Further, once the completed script has been delivered, no addition, alteration or omission may be made without both the author's and producer's consent.

The manner in which the screenwriter and the bookwriter are entitled to share in the commercial success of the movie or play again evidences the distinction between their respective positions. A successful screenwriter may receive several hundred thousand dollars as his guaranteed payment for writing a screenplay; less successful writers will receive a far lesser payment. The playwright most often will receive under $5,000 as his guaranteed compensation.

As contingent compensation, the bookwriter will receive a percentage of the gross weekly box office receipts derived from each company which presents the play. The payment is made whether or not the producer has made any profit from the play during that week. Gross weekly box office receipts are comprised of sales revenues from all sources in connection with the production of the play, less certain deductions, such as taxes imposed upon admissions, commissions paid in connection with theater parties or benefits and a percentage amount set aside for pension and welfare funds of theatrical unions. If the play is performed by more than one company, the percentage compensation accruing from each company is computed and paid separately.

In comparison, the screenwriter's contingent compensation is in the form of a percentage of the net profits derived from the motion picture. He may receive a percentage of 100 percent of the profits which are so derived or only that percentage of profits which is retained by the producer. Before a picture is deemed to be in profits, generally there will be deducted from the gross amount of revenues which the distributor receives a distribution fee, the costs and expenses of distribution, and the cost of producing the film, including overhead charges and interest. The definition of net profits varies from contract to contract and is ordinarily the product of much negotiation.

The playwright and screenwriter both will profit handsomely from their contingent participations if the production is an extremely successful one. If it is not, generally the screenwriter will receive no income from his profit participation while the playwright, unless he waives his participation in gross box office receipts, will collect these sums so long as the play is running.

Those readers interested in an unusual and informative discussion of the computation of net profits are referred to a pamphlet entitled *Motion Picture Distribution: An Accountant's Perspective* by David J. Leedy. Regarding the agreement between the produer and playwright, a review of the Dramatists Guild Minimum Basic Production Contract is recommended.

The Collaboration Agreement Among Playwrights

Many creative endeavors are the product of collaborative efforts by two or more creators. In all such cases, it is desirable for the prospective collaborators to agree among themselves at the outset as to their respective rights and obligations and to prepare an agreement confirming their understanding.

This article will focus on the issues to be addressed in a collaboration agreement among playwrights of a musical play containing a book, music and lyrics. The discussion also may be applicable to collaborations involving dramatic plays and other creative endeavors (such as books or records) in which more than one creator makes contributions.

The collaboration agreement should cover the following issues:

1. Who will contribute what elements to the collaborative effort? The agreement should set forth who will write what elements of the play (i.e., book, music and lyrics) and whether they will do so individually or jointly. If a deadline or work schedule for the completion of various elements has been agreed to, this should be set forth.

2. Who will own the copyright in the various elements of the play? The copyright in each separate element may be held by the creator(s) of that element. Alternatively, the copyright in the entire play may be held jointly by all the authors collectively. The resolution of this issue may affect the transfer of rights in the play, although the authors may agree in the collaboration agreement as to appropriate restrictions on the exercise of rights in the separate elements. (See the discussion on merger below.)

3. Are the book, music and lyrics all original, or is any element of the play based on any underlying material? If any collaborator has furnished underlying material (for

125

example, a novel written by such collaborator or a novel as to which such collaborator has acquired a dramatization rights option), the agreement should provide for an appropriate license or assignment to the collaborators of the dramatization rights in the underlying material. Of course, in most instances when plays are based upon underlying material, the producer will have acquired the dramatization rights.

4. How will the proceeds derived from the play be shared? Among the questions relating to this issue are the following:

    a.   How will royalties and other monies derived from the production of the play be shared? Will each author receive an equal share, or will the shares differ by virtue of the different contributions made by the various authors, the underlying material controlled by one or more of them, the relative prominence of the authors, or other factors?

    b.   Have the authors agreed on any minimum level of royalties payable to them individually or collectively with respect to a first-class or other production (for example, no less than two percent to each of the bookwriter, composer and lyricist)?

    c.   What will be the division of proceeds from the disposition of subsidiary rights in the play? Generally, the division will be in the same proportion as the sharing of royalties from stage presentations, but there are variations. In addition, the authors may wish to provide for certain limitations on the producer's and director's sharing in subsidiary rights or may wish to provide for a floor that will accrue to the authors after all third-party participations have been paid (Ordinarily, the producer of a first-class production will be entitled to receive 40 percent of the net receipts derived from the disposition of certain subsidiary rights after a certain number of first-class performances.)

5. How will the music publishing rights in the music and lyrics of the play be treated? Generally, the music pub-

lishing rights in the music and lyrics, including publication, mechanical reproduction, synchronization and small performing rights, are not considered subsidiary rights in the play but are reserved to the composer and lyricist. It is common, however, for the collaboration agreement to impose certain restrictions on the exercise of synchronization rights by the composer and lyricist and their music publishers.

6. Who will have the power to make creative decisions and exercise artistic approvals? In the Minimum Basic Production Contract and most other theatrical production contracts, the authors collectively have a right of approval over the cast, director and certain other creative personnel and also over any changes made in the play. The collaboration agreement should provide how such approvals will be exercised. For example, creative decisions could be made by a majority vote of the authors, either in interest or in number. Alternatively, each author could have an exclusive right of approval with respect to the elements of the play created by him, or unanimous approval could be required for all decisions. The agreement might also provide that after the completion of the play, no party shall make any change or alteration in the play without the others' consent.

7. Who will have the authority to control dispositions of rights in the play? Again, decisions may be made by a numerical majority, by a majority in interest, by unanimous consent, or on some other basis. The agreement may also provide that no party will require as a condition of granting his approval that he be engaged in another capacity (e.g., as an actor in the production). It will ordinarily specify that each party will keep the others fully informed of the progress of all negotiations relating to production contracts or the disposition of rights in the play.

8. Do all authors have to sign all agreements for the disposition of rights in the play, or can those with a majority in interest or a numerical majority bind the others? It is often helpful for a party to grant to one of the other

authors or to a third party the right to execute documents
if he is unavailable. The agreement should provide for a
fully executed copy of each contract to be sent to each
of the authors.

9.   What happens if an author dies? Ordinarily, the proceeds
     payable to him thereafter would be payable to his estate.
     Will the surviving authors, however, have the sole right
     to make changes in the play and to exercise other creative
     approvals or to negotiate and contract for the disposition
     of rights in the play, or should the deceased author's
     estate play a role in this?

10. What rights will any of the authors have with respect to
     replacing any of the other authors or bringing in new
     creators? What rights will a replaced author have? It is
     desirable for the collaboration agreement to provide for
     such contingencies in the event that the collaborators have
     creative differences or one of them is unwilling or unable
     to do the necessary work to complete the play.

11. What form of credit will the authors be entitled to receive?
     Ordinarily, there are separate authorship credits for the
     book, music and lyrics. The authors should agree in ad-
     vance on the form, size, order and placement of the credits
     and the media in which they should appear.

12. Will any of the authors perform other services in con-
     nection with the play—e.g., as director or as performer?
     If so, the agreement should specify whether the compen-
     sation for such services will be payable solely to the in-
     dividual author or whether it will be shared with the
     others. As noted above, the authors may wish to prohibit
     any one of them from requiring that he be engaged in
     some other capacity as a condition of granting approval
     or exercising other rights under the collaboration agree-
     ment.

13. What rights, if any, do the authors have to sell, pledge
     or assign their interests in the play? If such interests are
     assignable, the collaboration agreement may provide that
     the other authors have a right of first negotiation and/
     or first refusal to acquire them before they may be sold
     or assigned to any unrelated third party.

14. Do any of the authors have agents, and are there any special provisions regarding agency? The agreement may provide that the authors mutually may select one agent to represent the play and to receive a commission on each author's share. It may also specify that each author shall have the right to select his own agent with respect to his interest in the play, provided that such agent shall be commissionable only on that author's share of the proceeds.

15. Do expenses to be incurred by the authors require the approval of the other authors? Are they to be shared according to the percentage of interest of the parties or in some other manner? The agreement may provide that expenses incurred by individual authors in connection with the play be recoupable from the first proceeds received by the authors from the play. Expenses incurred in connection with the separate music and lyrics ordinarily should be borne solely by the composer and lyricist.

16. Will there be a merger of rights in the play? Some collaboration agreements provide that if the play is presented for a certain number of first-class performances, the rights in the book, music and lyrics (other than the music publishing rights in the music and lyrics and publication rights in the book) will merge, and that thereafter no disposition of any rights in any element of the play may be made except as a part of a disposition of rights in the merged play. The production contract with the producer frequently will provide for such a merger after the play has run for a certain number of performances, even if the collaboration agreement does not, in order to protect the producer's rights in the play.

17. What is the term of the agreement? Generally, this either will be for the life of the copyright in the play or in perpetuity. However, the agreement may provide for an earlier termination if certain conditions are not met—e.g., if the play has not been substantially completed by a certain date or if the parties have not entered into a production contract by a certain date. The agreement may provide that in the event of such a termination, the col-

laborators separately will own the elements of the play created by them.

18.   What rights do the authors have with respect to material not used in the play? The agreement may provide that such material, or material deleted from the play before a certain number of performances, shall be owned by the authors of such material, but that the use of such material in other media may be restricted (e.g., to prohibit references to characters used in the play or to the title of the play in the use of any such material).

19.   What warranties, representations and indemnities will be included? Ordinarily, each author will warrant and represent that the contributions made by him are wholly original and do not contain any material which is libelous, obscene, an invasion of privacy, an infringement of copyright, a violation of the right of publicity, or is otherwise unlawful or in violation of the rights of any third party. Ordinarily, each author will agree to indemnify the others with respect to any breach of any representation, warranty or agreement made by such author. If any author has furnished any underlying material for the play, or if there are any real persons or incidents depicted, counsel should make sure that all appropriate rights and clearances have been obtained and that the parties furnishing such material or clearances make appropriate representations and warranties. The collaboration agreement also may specify the manner in which the defense of any claim is to be handled.

20.   How are disputes to be resolved? It is often helpful to include an arbitration clause for resolving disputes among the authors.

21.   Are there any special provisions regarding the initial production of the play? The agreement may provide, for example, that in the event of a first-class producton, the Dramatists Guild Minimum Basic Production Contract form will be used.

The agreement should also set forth the parties' understanding, if any, regarding miscellaneous issues such as house seats, notices, and what jurisdiction's law will apply.

Of course, the provisions of a collaboration agreement are subject to modification by the authors at a later time if, in the course of negotiations with producers or otherwise, they wish to change their initial understanding. The preparation of such an agreement at the earliest possible time, however, will serve to avoid many potential problems and will help ensure that the authors concentrate on the creative aspects of their collaboration.

The Pre-Sale and Its Problems

Although the percentage of successful to unsuccessful investments in motion pictures, as measured by almost all standards, remains small, the enormous profits generated by a successful picture together with other tangible and intangible factors, lure to the motion picture production arena large numbers of producers and packagers. Because funds available from the traditional source of capital, the production/distribution company (herein called the "Distributor"), are not nearly sufficient to meet the demand, and because one is able to obtain more favorable terms of distribution by obtaining some or all of his financing from a source other than the Distributor, new sources and methods of financing are constantly sought.

In return for providing a stipulated amount of financing for the picture, which financing is usually made available at periodic intervals and under strict controls, the Distributor will be granted exclusive rights to distribute the picture in certain territories (sometimes the world). The monies remitted to the Distributor from the exhibitors of the picture customarily will be applied as follows: first, the Distributor will deduct and retain for itself a distribution fee; second, the Distributor will recoup its expenses of distributing the picture; third, the Distributor will recoup the amount which it provided to finance the picture, which will include an overhead factor and will bear interest; and fourth, the remainder, constituting profits, will be divided between the producer and the Distributor on some predetermined basis.

The foregoing, of course, represents a brief outline of a complicated and lengthy agreement.

The result, sought by producers who obtain financing from sources other than the Distributor, is to enter into a "gross deal" which provides that the Distributor will pay to the producer a percentage of all amounts received by the Distributor from the first dollar so received. Distribution fees and expenses will be borne by the Distributor from the percentage of receipts which it retains.

133

One desirable way for a producer to obtain financing other than from the Distributor is to seek same from persons, firms and corporations, either through private or public offerings. Frequently, the investor will purchase an interest as a limited partner in a limited partnership and will assume no liabilities in excess of his capital contribution. Often the general partner will be the producer who will have control over the production of the picture. When the picture is completed, the limited partnership will attempt to enter into an agreement (hopefully a "gross deal") with a Distributor, and the monies remitted to the limited partnership will be shared by the general and limited partners after the expenses of the limited partnership have been paid and the capital contributions of the limited partners have been repaid.

The limited partnership was the vehicle most frequently used in connection with tax sheltered investments, usually in the form of amortization arrangements and production service arrangements, which emerged in the United States several years ago and were a significant factor in motion picture production until Internal Revenue Service rulings left them battered, though not totally eliminated.

Producers who control packages (a term which refers to the underlying property on which the picture is to be based together with several key elements such as the director and the lead performers) which have worldwide appeal have been able to obtain a portion of the required financing in advance of production by granting distribution rights on a territory by territory basis to distributors in each such territory and obtaining advance payments from these distributors. Thus, the producer may grant to a French distributor the exclusive rights to distribute the picture in France and be paid, in stages, an advance against his share of distribution revenues or he may make an outright sale of distribution rights in a particular territory for a specific sum of money. If the producer were able to finance the picture in this manner without disposing of distribution rights in the United States, he then would be in a position at the appropriate time to negotiate a strong agreement with the United States Distributor.

Another method of obtaining pre-sale financing is to dispose of television (including pay-television) and other rights prior to production of the picture. The normal sequence of motion film exploitation commences with the exhibition of the picture in theaters shortly after the picture has been completed. Then for a period of time the picture is licensed for transmission on pay television, following which time the picture will be broadcast on network television. When the network run is completed, the picture will be licensed to a television syndicator, generally to be sold in a group with other pictures on a market by market basis.

If a picture is successful theatrically, it is reasonable to expect that either or both of a free television or pay television network will pay a significant amount for the exhibition rights.

Realizing this, producers in need of financing and possessing a strong package have been able to convince potential television licensees to agree in advance of production to purchase the rights to exhibit the picture. The inducement to the licensee is that it may be purchasing at a bargain price a picture which ultimately may be commercially successful, and further, the licensee need not pay the bulk of the purchase price until the picture is available to it for exhibition. Because of this latter factor regarding the time of payment, the producer must then attempt to discount his license agreement with a financier, a process which when completed may yield to the producer for purposes of production financing far less than the face value of the amount specified in the agreement.

Because these license agreements generally are with one of three free television networks and one or two pay and syndication companies, all of which at present are financially sound, there has been little difficulty convincing the lender that the obligations contained in the license agreement are backed by a financially responsible party. Yet, the lender who discounts the license agreements usually will demand that the first monies generated from exploitation of the film be applied in repayment of its loan. A producer seeking outside investors and a favorable arrangement with a completion guarantor may be hindered by this requirement. Also, many lenders are not willing to take as the only collateral security for their loan the negative of the picture and the various contracts to which the producer is a party. Often a personal guarantee of repayment by the producer, especially an independent one, will be sought.

Lenders have been troubled by a provision frequently contained in the network license agreement which allows the network to reject the picture if it does not conform to network Standards and Practices. Because the decision to reject is partially a subjective one, a lender has no absolute assurance that the network will accept the picture; hence no guarantee that the collateral afforded to the lender by the network agreement is secure. Further, if the network refuses to accept the picture, the probability is that the pay and syndication companies also will refuse.

Producers are meeting this problem by shooting two versions of potentially offensive scenes. They also are working closely with network executives, submitting to them prior to and during shooting proposed revisions of the screenplay for evaluation by the Standards and Practices department.

There is substantial incentive for producers to satisfy these problems; for the pre-sale provides one of the few aids to the producer who chooses or is forced to finance a motion picture without the use of major studio financing.

Financing Stage Plays

The Securities and Exchange Commission ("SEC") has adopted new rules concerning private offerings of securities and rescinded others which had previously been in effect. These new rules, collectively known as Regulation D, became effective April 15, 1982, and have begun to be used for the raising of money for live theatrical productions. In addition, over the past year and a half there have been changes in the New York law and regulations applicable to theatrical financings.

This discussion will highlight alternative means that may be available to a theatrical producer who is seeking to raise funds. It is not exhaustive, and in each instance when representing a producer, the attorney should review in depth all applicable statutes and regulations.

The form of business entity that is almost always used to finance theatrical productions is the limited partnership. When such a partnership is based in New York or is formed to finance a play to be produced in New York, it will generally be subject to the requirements of the New York limited partnership law.[1]

The limited partnership has several advantages over other forms of business organizations in connection with the financing of plays. First, an investor's liability generally is limited to the amount of his contributions to the partnership.[2] An investor, however, may authorize his contribution to be used by the general partner for production or pre-production purposes prior to full capitalization of the partnership, in which event there is a risk that he may sustain unlimited liability for all debts arising prior to formation of the limited partnership. Second, it will generally be possible for the limited partners to treat financial losses for federal income tax purposes as ordinary rather than capital losses and to deduct such losses against ordinary income. Because the majority of production entities formed to produce plays lose money, this is a major advantage for investors. Third, the general partner will have virtually complete control over the partnership's activities.

Other forms of business entities have been used to finance the production of plays (a case in point being the Broadway production of "The Little Prince," which was financed through the sale to the public of 750,000 shares of a newly formed corporation at an offering price of two dollars each), but in view of the advantages of the limited partnership, this form of organization is almost universally used.

In New York, a limited partnership is formed by the filing of a limited partnership certificate which must include information specified by statute.[3] It is beyond the scope of this article to detail the requirements of New York and federal law concerning limited partnerships and their tax treatment, but one statutory change, particularly relevant to theatrical productions, is worth noting. In June, 1981, the legal requirement of newspaper publication of public notice of the formation of a limited partnership for financing a theatrical production was eliminated, so long as the words "limited partnership" appear in the name of the limited partnership syndication.[4] To avoid the requirement and expense of publication, therefore, the words "limited partnership" should be included in the name of any partnership formed to produce a play.

In New York, as in other states and on the federal level, the offering of interests in a limited partnership is considered an offering of "securities" and is subject to governmental regulation. The financing of theatrical productions in New York is regulated by the New York Theatrical Syndication Financing Act[5] and by regulations of the state Attorney General issued pursuant thereto.[6] Unless an offering falls within one of the exceptions referred to below, an issuer may raise money for a theatrical production only by means of an offering circular or a prospectus setting forth detailed information required by the regulations, including details regarding the production entity, the producers, and agreements with third parties to acquire rights or services to be used in connection with the play.

There are several categories of offerings in which it is not necessary to prepare a separate offering circular to be reviewed by the Attorney General:

(1) When a prospectus as part of a registration statement or an offering circular pursuant to Regulation A (discussed below) has been cleared by the SEC, such offering literature may be used in New York.[7]

(2) When the offering was made as a private placement pursuant to former Rule 146 under the Securities Act of 1933, a private placement memorandum in the form prescribed by the Attorney General could be used.[8]

(3) When the offering is for $250,000 or less, the issuer may file an investment agreement clearly setting forth the terms of the offering in lieu of a prospectus or offering circular.[9]

(4) When an offering is made to fewer than 36 persons and each investor signs an express waiver of the offering circular requirements, the issuer need only file the original waiver forms, two copies of the investment agreement and one copy of the certificate of limited partnership, together with a copy of all contracts and options with authors and a representation by the producers that they have no knowledge or belief that the offering was made to more than 35 offerees and that they do not know of any investors represented by nominees other than those listed on the waivers. These materials must be filed with the Attorney General no later than the first paid public performance of the production.[10] The Attorney General must also be notified of a producer's intent to proceed by means of waivers within 30 days of the initial receipt of monies (other than "front money") from an investor. The waiver procedure is not limited by the dollar amount of the offering, but it is important to note that it applies only to offerings made to fewer than 36 offerees as opposed to purchasers.

A further exemption from the normal disclosure requirements is available for a producer who seeks "front money" from fewer than five persons. "Front money" refers to funds which may be used only for certain specified pre-production expenses, including fees and advances for the purpose of purchasing options on a play, engaging creative personnel, securing a theater, and retaining legal and other professional advisors. The Attorney General's office has interpreted this provision not to apply to funds used to present a workshop or showcase presentation of a play while it is being developed.

The Attorney General has prescribed certain requirements with which all limited partnership agreements and other documents used for obtaining theatrical financing in New York must comply. Among these are that the minimum and maximum capitalization to be raised be set forth in the offering document, and the minimum must be no less than 75 percent of the maximum capitalizaton.[12] The offering document must also provide that all funds derived from the sale of theatrical syndication interest shall be held in trust in a special bank account.

The regulations prescribe the filing requirements and time periods for the Attorney General to review papers filed with it and to notify the issuer of any deficiencies to be corrected. They also set forth detailed accounting requirements concerning financial reports to be made to the investors and the Attorney General. The Attorney General may, upon the producer's application, grant an exemption from the accounting requirements for theatrical syndications offered to fewer than 36 persons or with a total capitalization of less than $250,000.[13]

At the federal level, the Securities Act of 1933 (the "Securities Act")[14] requires that all offerings other than those which are purely intrastate or those which fall within certain specified exemptions be made pursuant to a registration statement which meets the statutory requirements. The exemption for intrastate transactions applies solely to securities which are part of an issue offered and sold only to persons resident within a single state, where the issuer is a person resident and doing business within such state.[15]

Unless an exemption from registration is available, an issuer of interests in a theatrical syndication, like an issuer of any other securities, must file a registration statement with the SEC and have it cleared. A full registration entails the use of the S-1 registration form, which must set forth a great deal of information. A somewhat simplified registration form, S-18, may be used by limited partnerships for offerings not exceeding $5 million.[16] Once fully registered, the issuer becomes subject to the reporting requirements of the Securities and Exchange Act of 1934.[17] The cost involved make such a registration prohibitive for all except high-budget theatrical productions for which no exemption from registration is available.

There are four categories of exemptions from registration which are potentially available to theatrical producers, two of which are statutory and two of which are based on SEC rules. These are: (i) Section 4(2) of the Securities Act; (ii) Section 4(6) of the Securities

Act; (iii) Regulation A under the Securities Act; and (iv) Regulation D under the Securities Act. Each of these is examined briefly below.

Section 4(2) of the Securities Act[18] exempts "transactions by an issuer not involving any public offering" and constitutes the primary statutory basis for the private placement of securities. The courts and the SEC have interpreted this exemption to be available for offerings to persons who have access to the same type of information that registration would provide and who are able to fend for themselves. The burden is on the issuer to establish the availability of this exemption (and all other exemptions).[19] This exemption has not frequently been relied upon in theatrical financings, partially because of the indefiniteness of the statutory language for its use.

Section 4(6) of the Securities Act[20] exempts transactions in which offers of less than $5 million in securities are made solely to "accredited investors" and in which there is no advertising or public solicitation, if the issuer files a prescribed notice with the SEC. "Accredited investors" were defined by statute to include certain institutions as well as persons meeting standards of financial sophistication, net worth, knowledge and assets to be prescribed by the SEC.[21] In adopting Regulation D, the SEC defined "accredited investors" to include the following groups of persons who might invest in a theatrical limited partnership: certain institutional investors; general partners of the limited partnership, as well as directors and executive officers of those general partners; persons purchasing at least $150,000 of the securities, if the purchase price does not exceed 20 percent of the investor's and spouse's combined net worth at the time of sale; natural persons whose net worth (with spouse) is at least $1 million; and natural persons whose income exceeded $200,000 in each of the last two years and who reasonably expect their income to exceed $200,000 in the current year. (The term "income" is not defined in the Regulation.)

Accordingly, the Section 4(6) exemption may be available to a theatrical producer who can restrict both offers and purchases to "accredited investors." There is no limitation on the number of purchasers pursuant to this section so long as all offerees and purchasers are accredited investors.

Regulation A[22] was adopted by the SEC pursuant to its statutory authority to exempt issues which are relatively small in amount or limited in character.[23] The Regulation provides an exemption from the full registration requirements for offerings aggregating $1,500,000 or less over a 12-month period. There are no restrictions on the number or qualifications of investors.

An issuer wishing to raise funds under Regulation A must file an offering statement with the SEC containing a notification, an offering circular and certain exhibits. Although these documents must contain detailed information prescribed in the Regulation, this procedure has several advantages over a full registration on Form S-1 or S-18. The offering statement may be filed in the New York regional office of the SEC and is likely to be cleared much more quickly than an S-1 or S-18 registration. The information required to be set forth is less extensive, and certified financial statements are not required unless the issuer is already reporting to the SEC. The issuer does not become subject to certain civil liabilities or to the reporting requirements triggered by a full registration.

Regulation A is frequently used by theatrical producers who do not need to raise more than $1,500,000. It offers flexibility in raising funds across state lines, and some states, including New York, will accept offering documents cleared by the SEC pursuant to Regulation A in satisfaction of their own Blue Sky requirements. It should be noted that the offering documents must not imply that the SEC approves any statement contained in them or the merits of the securities offered, and the SEC's review is directed only towards ensuring that the requirements of the Regulation are met. In addition, periodic reports of sales must be made to the SEC in order for the exemption to continue in effect.

Regulation D,[24] effective as of April 15, 1982, consists of Rules (501 through 506). The SEC's purpose in adopting the new rules was to simplify and broaden existing exemptions, to eliminate "unnecessary restrictions" on small issuers, and to achieve greater uniformity between federal and state exemptions. In furtherance of this purpose, the new rules have expanded the range of offerings entitled to exemption from registration.

Rules 504 through 506 establish three new exemptions from the registration requirements of the Securities Act and replace three other rules which were rescinded. Rule 504, which replaces Rule 240, provides an exemption for certain offers and sales aggregating $500,000 or less within a 12-month period. There is no limit on the number of investors to whom securities may be sold under Rule

504. The Rule does not set forth any specific disclosure requirements regarding information to be furnished to investors but does make it clear that the issuer will continue to be subject to the antifraud and civil liability provisions of the Securities Act. With certain exceptions, no general solicitation of offerings (such as by means of newspaper advertisements) under Rule 504 is permitted. The use of Rule 504 may be considered by theatrical producers seeking to raise no more than $500,000.

Rule 505, which replaces Rule 242, provides an exemption for offers and sales aggregating up to $5 million over a 12-month period to an unlimited number of accredited investors plus up to 35 purchasers who are not accredited investors. If an offering is made under Rule 505 only to accredited investors, then, as with Rule 504, no specific disclosure requirements are mandated. However, if securities are sold to any investors that are not accredited, then the same kind of information as required in Part I of Form S-18 (or another registration form available to the issuer) must be provided. Rule 505 does not require that purchasers possess any degree of financial sophistication.

Rule 507, which replaces Rule 146, relates to transactions deemed to be exempt under Section 4(2) of the Securities Act. A Rule 506 offering may be made in an unlimited dollar amount to any number of accredited investors plus up to 35 purchasers who are not accredited investors. The issuer must reasonably believe, prior to making any sale, that each purchaser who is not an accredited investor, either alone or with his purchaser representative, has such knowledge and experience in financial and business matters that he is capable of evaluating the merits and risks of the prospective investment. Thus, in an offering under Rule 506, it is important to inquire as to the investment sophistication of prospective purchasers and their representatives. As compared with rescinded Rule 146, Rule 506 requires a determination that only purchasers, and not offerees, meet the sophistication standard. In addition, the "economic risk" test under Rule 146 has been eliminated. The disclosure requirements are the same as under Rule 505, and no general solicitation may take place.

Rule 503 of Regulation D requires that periodic notices be filed with the SEC on a prescribed form. In addition, all offerings under the regulation are subject to the antifraud and civil liability provisions of the Securities Act and the Blue Sky laws of states in which the offerings are made.

Offers and sales of theatrical limited partnership interest must comply with the Blue Sky laws of all states in which offers or sales are made or in which purchasers reside. In this regard, some states may require a separate registration or filing in order for the securities to be offered in that state. In addition, it should be determined whether the issuer needs to qualify as a broker-dealer or engage a qualified broker-dealer to offer the securities in a particular state.

It is hoped that these vehicles for financing theatrical productions will provide greater flexibility in the raising of funds for new productions.

FOOTNOTES

1.   *McKinney's Consolidated Laws of New York, Annotated,* Art. 8, Sections 90 et seq.

2.   *Id.,* Section 96.

3.   *Id.,* Section 91.

4.   N.Y. General Business Law, Section 399-c(3a), as amended June 3, 1981.

5.   N.Y. General Business Law, Art. 26-A, Sections 399-b *et seq.*

6.   N.Y. Attorney General Regulations, Chapter III: Theatrical Syndication Financing, Part 50.

7.   *Id.,* Section 50.1(e).

8.   *Id.,* Section 50.1(f)(ii). It is believed that a private placement memorandum under Regulation D may be used as well if it conforms to the Attorney General's form.

9.   *Id.,* Section 50.1(f)(iii).

10.   *Id.,* Sections 50.1(g), 50.4(a)(iv).

11.   *Id.,* Section 50.1(i).

12.   *Id.,* Section 50.2(b)(5).

13.   N.Y. Attorney General Regulations, Theatrical Accounting, Part 51.

14.   15 U.S.C. Sections 77a *et seq.*

15.   15 U.S.C. Section 77c(a)(11).

16.   SEC Release No. 33-6406.

17.   15 U.S.C. Sections 78a *et seq.*
18.   15 U.S.C. Section 77d(2).
19.   *See* SEC v. Ralston Purina Co., 346 U.S. 119 (1953).
20.   15 U.S.C. Section 77d(6).
21.   15 U.S.C. Section 77b(15).
22.   17 CFR Sections 230.251 *et seq.*
23.   Securities Act, Section 3(b), 15 U.S.C. Section 77c(b).
24.   17 CFR Sections 230.501 - 230.506.

The Investment Tax Credit

One reason that a producer is willing to assume the financial risks inherent in the making of a motion picture or television production is the availability of the Investment Tax Credit (the "ITC"). Because of the significant impact of the ITC on production financing, an acquaintance with the highlights of the ITC is useful.

The ITC is a tax incentive that was passed by Congress to increase domestic employment. Taxpayers who purchase or produce certain types of assets may deduct from their federal income tax, up to specified limits, a percentage of the amount spent to acquire or manufacture such assets.

A new film created primarily for use as public entertainment or for educational purposes is an asset for which the ITC may be available.

However, any film or tape program for which the market is primarily topical or is otherwise transitory in nature is not eligible. Specific examples of excluded programs are television evening news shows and news specials relating to public affairs, award shows, game shows and shows of sporting events.

To be eligible for the ITC a taxpayer must possess "an ownership interest" in all or "a part of a film" at the time it is "placed in service."

A person has an ownership interest to the extent that he shares in any loss that may be incurred in respect of a film. The regulations of the Internal Revenue Service treat the taxpayer as having an ownership interest to the extent his capital is "at risk," and provide that his capital will be at risk to the extent that he will suffer economic loss if the film fails to generate sufficient revenue to cover or repay production costs.

A "part of a film" is defined as the exclusive right to display a film in one medium of exhibition in one geographical area over the entire period of substantial exploitation of the film.

147

A medium of exhibition is theatrical release, television release or any other medium of displaying a film, and a geographical area is a defined commercial market recognized by the motion picture or program industry, but which in no event may be smaller than one country.

Because a producer who furnishes a movie of the week to a television network ordinarily retains off-network syndication rights, the network does not acquire the exclusive right to display the film in one medium of exhibition, and thus the network does not acquire "a part" of the film. In such a circumstance, and provided other criteria are met, the ITC will belong to the producer. This despite the fact that the network may provide virtually all the financing for the production.

A film is placed in service when it is first exhibited or otherwise utilized before the primary audience for which it was created.

This provision has been criticized by some who feel that the determination should be based on the time when the film has been completed, rather than when a distributor or network decides to exhibit the film. This would be consistent with regulations relating to other types of property for which the ITC generally is available at the earlier of either the taxable year in which depreciation commences or the taxable year in which the property is placed in a condition or state of readiness and available for its specifically assigned function.

Generally, the amount of the ITC is 10 percent of the "qualified investment" that a taxpayer invests in the property. The "qualified investment" can be equal to 100 percent of the property's basis, although that percentage may vary depending upon the taxpayer's elections concerning depreciation of the film.

The ITC basis of a film is the amount of qualified United States production costs, which include all direct production costs of a film that are allocable to United States sources. In addition, all other costs of production of a film except direct production costs that are allocable to foreign sources, are included in the ITC basis if 80 percent or more of all direct production costs are allocable to sources in the United States.

Of interest is the regulation allowing the inclusion in production costs of residuals fixed by collective bargaining agreements and participations (to a limit) in gross or net income of the film.

To illustrate the benefit of the ITC, assume that a motion picture is produced by an independent producer who expended qualified U.S. production costs of $2 million. If that producer is allowed an ITC of 10 percent of such production costs, the result is that he may deduct from his federal income taxes $200,000.

Although the above represents a simplified outline, it is obvious that with proper tax planning and guidance a producer or investor can obtain significant advantages from the ITC.

Variety, October 15, 1980

The Motion Picture Turnaround Provision

During the course of negotiations between representatives of a producer and studio relating to the development of a motion picture, it is common for the studio to agree that if it abandons development of the picture, the producer will have the right for a period of time thereafter to place the property elsewhere. The clause embodying this concept is called a "turnaround" provision and it contains several elements.

The threshold question is, when will the property be deemed to have been abandoned? Some studios approach this issue by agreeing to provide notice to the producer when they elect to abandon the project. In the absence of a definition of abandonment, this, of course, is an open-ended provision.

Another approach allows the studio a specified period of time after the delivery of the final screenplay, the proposed negative cash budget and the commitment of the principal cast and director of the picture to elect either to produce or abandon the picture.

A further variation specifies that if at any time the picture is not in "active development" the producer can request that the studio recommence active development or abandon the picture, and within a period of time following that request the studio must do one or the other. "Active development" is defined at length and includes, without limitation, such activities as negotiating for the services of a key element of the picture, commissioning screenplay material, preparing a budget and seeking production financing.

When the picture is deemed abandoned the producer has a period of time—usually no less than six months nor more than a year—to acquire all rights of the studio in and to all materials relating to the picture by paying a specified amount (the "buy-out price"). Generally, the only warranty the studio will make in regard to this transaction is that it has not theretofore transferred, hypothecated or otherwise disposed of any of its right, title and interest in the picture.

The buy-out price typically will consist of (i) all direct costs and payments made by the studio relating to the picture, plus (ii) a supervisory or overhead fee (often 10 to 15 percent of the amount of section (i)) plus (iii) interest on the total of sections (i) and (ii).

In addition, the studio will require that it receive a percentage of the profits (generally 5 percent of 100 percent of net profits) of each motion picture which is produced based upon the property which it developed.

The producer's right to purchase the developed materials is not unconditional. He must deliver to the studio an agreement executed by a financially responsible third party approved by the studio assuming all of the studio's obligations relating to the picture and indemnifying the studio against any loss relating thereto.

Also, if prior to producer's paying the buy-out price (and in the case of some turnaround provisions, for 60 days following such payment), the producer introduces any new, or alters any existing elements of the picture and/or introduces any changed terms and conditions relating to the financial terms regarding the producer's involvement in the picture, he must advise the studio of these "changed elements." For a period of time thereafter, the studio has the right to elect to proceed with the development of production of the picture predicated on the use of these changed elements.

For example, if Studio A developed, then abandoned, the property and producer convinced Studio B to pay the buy-out price with the understanding that the picture would be produced using a director not previously involved in the project, Studio A first would have to be given the opportunity to develop or produce the project using the new director.

If, during the turnaround period the producer fails to exercise his option to pay the buy-out price, then his rights will terminate, and in some agreements it is provided that the studio no longer will have any obligation to use his services if it subsequently produces the picture.

Some provisions also specify that if producer commissions any additional writing to be done during the turnaround period, then following the expiration of that period the studio will have the right to acquire all of the producer's rights in and to such additional writing by paying his actual direct costs therefor.

If the project being developed is based on an underlying work, and during the turnaround period either the producer or the studio fails to exercise an option regarding that work, then the producer's turnaround rights will expire upon that failure. Several companies also provide that if the producer thereafter acquires any rights to such underlying work, he is deemed to hold same in trust until the studio shall have received the entire buy-out price.

Turnaround provisions are detailed and lengthy and prior to execution of an agreement with the producer, studios are somewhat inflexible in negotiating these clauses. When the turnaround period begins, however, studios sometimes are willing to make adjustments such as allowing the producer to pay an option price which enables him to develop the property for a period of time (by obtaining rewrites of the screenplay or a key element such as a director) without then having to pay the buy-out price. Prior to the expiration of the option period, the producer either must pay the buy-out price or all rights, including rights to any newly written material, revert to the studio. Such an arrangement also contemplates that the studio will waive the "changed elements" provision in order to enable the producer to add a key element.

Further, in these negotiations, the studio sometimes is willing to reduce the amount of its profit participation.

However, there is no assurance that any such variations will be obtained, and accordingly, the producer's representative should attempt to negotiate as fully as possible all aspects of the turnaround provision prior to execution of the agreement.

Ancillary Rights in Motion Pictures

Ancillary or subsidiary exploitations are those designed to support the primary use, which in the case of motion pictures is in domestic and foreign theaters. During the last several years, revenues derived from ancillary sources have increased in relation to those derived from the primary source, resulting in changes in the way producers approach the production and exploitation of feature films.

In 1977, domestic theatrical rentals accounted for approximately 52 percent of the total revenues of a motion picture and foreign rentals provided an additional 30 percent. In 1982, the corresponding percentages were 42 and 17. During that same period of time the percentage of total revenues derived from home video (videocassettes and videodiscs) rose from negligible to 8 percent and revenues derived from pay television leaped from 1½ percent to 17½ percent.

Even more noteworthy is the prediction contained in a study undertaken by RCA Corp. (the "RCA Study") which hypothesizes that by 1990 revenues from pay television will soar to $16.3 billion, approximately three times the estimated theatrical box office receipts at that time.

Such predictions are of concern to major motion picture companies which share in a greater percentage of box office receipts than they do in ancillary revenues. For example, the distributor receives approximately 50 percent of theatrical box office receipts but only 17 to 22 percent of pay television revenues. The latter percentage occurs because the cable operator remits to the pay system 50 percent or less of the fees paid by the subscriber who receives the pay service.

To obtain these ancillary sources of film revenue more quickly than in the past, as well as to avoid the diminution in the value of their product which results from the widespread pirating of copies of motion pictures, distributors have reduced the time period during which most films are kept in initial theatrical release. Similarly,

155

fewer films than in previous years are re-released for theatrical exhibition after their initial run.

Approximately three or four months after the initial theatrical release, the motion picture will be sold or rented to the public by means of videocassettes and videodiscs. The RCA Study postulates that consumer spending for home video software will increase from $500 million to $6.2 billion during the next eight years.

The market for home video software is larger in some foreign territories than the United States owing, in some measure, to the less varied fare available on free television in these territories. Some experts have speculated that the growth of the home video market in foreign territories will result in videocassette exploitation of a film becoming the primary, rather than a subsidiary market.

The pay television "window" of approximately 12 to 18 months occurs nine months to a year after the theatrical release, followed by broadcast on free network and syndicated television, the next two markets which are met as the film makes its way through the release pattern.

Although the prime time audience for the television networks has been decreasing in recent years and, according to the RCA Study, will continue to do so (from 80 percent at present to 66 percent in 1990), the number of television households is expected to increase to over 96 million by 1990. Accordingly, even though the networks are reluctant to pay exorbitant amounts for motion pictures which previously were transmitted on pay television, it is apparent that the free television marketplace will continue to provide significant revenues to distributors of films.

An ancillary market that may become a primary one is pay-per-view television. This market, in which the viewer pays a specific charge for each event which he watches, is regarded with great expectation by motion picture distributors, but has proved disappointing thus far.

Those films exhibited to date on pay-per-view have been ordered by only 10 to 25 percent of the subscribers capable of receiving this technology. The supporters of this medium, however, point to the time when available hardware which allows subscribers to order a film on impulse is in the homes of several million people who will pay five to ten dollars per household to watch a designated film. Such possible revenues coupled with the elimination of the need to duplicate in excess of a thousand prints for in excess of a thousand dollars each enables distributors to contemplate the time when they initially release a major motion picture by means of pay-per-view rather than in theaters.

All of the foregoing ancillary uses involve exploiting the motion picture in the form in which it originally was produced. Separate elements of the film also can be sources of revenue.

Films such as "Star Wars" and "E.T." exemplify the immense revenues which can be derived from a successful merchandising campaign. In addition to the traditional products and services to which are attached the names and/or likenesses of the films and the characters therein, new commercial tie-in possibilities are being developed. It has been reported, for example, that one company guaranteed the owner of the rights to "E.T." $21 million for the right to use that name in connection with videogames.

Films such as "Grease," "Saturday Night Fever" and "Chariots of Fire" illustrate the fact that music publishing revenues and soundtrack album royalties also may provide substantial income. When a classic composition emerges from such a film, the income may continue well beyond the life of the picture.

Finally, novelizations derived from screenplays, or books describing the making of a particular picture on occasion have brought income to the film producer. Even when the owner of the film does not have control over the disposition of these rights, he may derive income by licensing rights to the artwork from the film which is used in connection with the applicable book.

Although the potential revenues from ancillary sources have been cited to support the theory that there is less risk in financing feature films today than in previous years, it is still generally the case that the best insurance of success in the ancillary markets is a successful theatrical run. If subsidiary rights such as pay television become the tail that wags the motion picture dog, this axiom will be subject to change.

Summary of Speech for American Bar Association Forum Committee on Entertainment and Sports Industries, March 18, 1983 (published in *New York Law Journal).*

First Negotiation, First Refusal, Option

A news article has stated that a major motion picture company, for its investment in a musical play, will receive among other benefits, a right of first negotiation for the motion picture rights. A discussion of the relationship among the rights of "first negotiation," "first refusal" and "option" is helpful in analyzing what the company did and did not acquire and the precision required when using these terms.

The report described the right obtained by the company as "the exclusive right to meet whatever price is set for the film rights by the authors." It did not elaborate on the specific aspects of the right, such as what occurs once the authors set a price, for how long and in what form must negotiations take place and what happens if the parties are not able to agree?

Typically an author who grants to a company a right of first negotiation for motion picture rights agrees that if he ever intends to dispose of these rights he will negotiate with the company prior to negotiating with any third party. The contract will specify a period of time during which *bona fide* negotiations must take place. If at the end of this period the parties are not able to agree, the author may then conduct negotiations with any other entity and one of the following situations will apply:

(1) the author will be free to enter into an agreement for the rights in question regardless of whether the terms are more or less favorable to him than those last offered by the company. In this situation, all that the company has bargained for is a right to be persuasive before the offers of others are submitted; or

(2) the company will have the right of first refusal to meet an offer of a third party. (Sometimes this right is referred to as "last refusal").

A right of first refusal may be coupled with, or exist independently from, a right of first negotiation. Generally it provides that if the author at any time receives an offer to sell the motion picture rights, which offer he wishes to accept, he must advise the company of the name of the offeror and the terms and conditions of the offer. After receiving that notice, the company will have a certain period of time in which to notify the author that it will acquire the rights on the terms specified in that offer. If the company does not elect to do so, the author, during a designated time period thereafter, may sell the rights to the person who made the offer, but only on terms at least as favorable to author as those contained in the offer. If the author elects to sell the rights on terms less favorable than those contained in the original notice to the company, he again must offer company the right to meet those less favorable terms.

The right of first refusal, although more favorable to the company than a right of first negotiation, nevertheless exposes the company to the uncertainties of a third party offer.

An option contract eliminates these uncertainties by specifying a time period during which the company may elect to acquire motion picture rights on terms and conditions which previously have been agreed upon. These are set forth in an agreement which is undated and attached to the option contract. If and when the company elects to exercise its option, no further negotiations are necessary because the contract automatically will become operative and be dated appropriately.

It should be noted that the rights referred to in this article are not confined to the acquisition of motion picture rights, but are commonly utilized in all fields of entertainment.

Variety, February 28, 1979

After the Broadway Run—The Tams-Witmark Settlement

The stipulation of settlement in a class action suit brought by certain owners and operators of dinner theaters, musical theaters, playhouses and others against Tams-Witmark Music Library, Inc. ("Tams")[1] is informative to those who are involved in the musical theater.

Most plays which are presented on Broadway are governed by the terms of a Minimum Basic Production Agreement which specifies basic terms agreed upon between the Dramatists Guild and producers. That agreement covers first-class productions of the play and allows the author, subject to certain restrictions and to certain possible participations by producers in revenues, to dispose of so-called stock and amateur rights in and to the play.

According to the plaintiffs, over the last 50 years Tams has acquired from authors of various Broadway musicals the right to license approximately 60 percent of all desirable musicals available for use after their Broadway runs. The authors of such musicals as "My Fair Lady," "Hello Dolly," "Promises, Promises," "Man of La Mancha," "Mame," "Cabaret," "Sweet Charity" and "Gypsy" have granted to Tams licensing rights in and to those plays.

Frequently Tams is granted the right to license performances of the play after the close of the producer's continuous first-class road tour of the play, but in no event later than a specified time period following the close of the Broadway run. The duration of the agreement often is for the full term of copyright in the applicable elements constituting the play.

For its services, Tams receives a percentage commission of all gross sums which are derived as a result of licensing stock and amateur rights to the play. A 10 percent commission for licenses of stock performance rights and a 20 percent commission for licenses of amateur performance rights are not unusual. Tams may pay an advance amount to be applied against any sums which become due

161

to the author (and any other participant in revenues from the play).

Tams will be granted the right to make copies of materials such as the prompt book, dialogue sets, vocal and choral parts, piano-conductor score and orchestra parts of the play. Copies of these materials are provided by Tams for a rental charge to its licensees. Sometimes, in the license agreement between the author and Tams, the weekly rental charge which Tams may exact is limited; this rental charge apparently is retained entirely by Tams.

After it has acquired the rights to a particular play, Tams will include that play in its catalogue and endeavor to license to dinner theaters, musical theaters, playhouses and other licensees the rights to present the play. The license agreement will specify the duration of the license and provide that the licensee pay to Tams minimum guaranteed royalties either against a specified percentage of gross box office receipts or plus a specified percentage of such receipts in excess of a pre-determined amount. As noted above, the licensee rents from Tams the musical material for the preparation and completion of the performances of the play and pays to Tams a weekly rental charge for this material. The licensee is restricted from copying, reproducing, selling or otherwise distributing any such materials and is required to return same to Tams promptly following the last performance of the play. It is not unusual that Tams requires that the full rental fee plus a specified amount representing security for the safe return of the material all be paid to Tams on execution of the agreement.

The licensee is required to preserve faithfully in all performances the story, plot and form of the play as written and must agree to make no additions or changes of any kind in the music score or the book except as may specifically be authorized in writing by the author.

Over the years Tams has concerned itself with the acquisition of musicals only, leaving the market for dramatic plays to Samuel French, Inc. and Dramatists Play Service, Inc., the significant licensors of dramatic plays in the country.

Chateau de Ville Productions, Inc., Westbury Music Fair, Inc. and several other dinner theaters and operators brought a class action suit against Tams asking for damages and injunctive relief on allegations that Tams violated Sections 1 and 2 of the Sherman Anti-Trust Act and Section 7 of the Clayton Act through various business practices designed to restrain competition in the licensing and performance of copyrighted musicals. In addition to citing the acquisition by Tams of approximately 60 percent of all desirable musicals available for use after their Broadway runs, plaintiffs alledged that because the rights acquired by Tams are exclusive and extend for the life of copyright, theaters cannot obtain the rights to such musicals obtained by Tams from anyone other than Tams, even from the authors.

In support of its claim, plaintiffs noted that of the approximately 160 dinner theaters in the United States, approximately 100 have presented musicals licensed from Tams. They estimated that over 300 musical theaters in the country have dealt with Tams.

The class action was concerned only with productions of musicals licensed by Tams for presentation by substantially professional casts before paying audiences; it was not concerned with such users as high schools, church groups and similar organizations.

Among the items complained of by plaintiffs were the following:

"As a result of Tams' control over the market for musicals, licensees must obtain rights from Tams at excessive fees and on a take-it-or-leave-it basis. Thus, when charging on the basis of a percentage of receipts, Tams requires licensees to ascribe to its definition of gross receipts, requires excessive and unwarranted license fees and royalties and substantial advance payments well before the time the musical is presented. In addition, it requires minimum guaranteed license fees. Moreover, all licensees must rent musical materials such as scripts, scores and orchestrations from Tams with each musical at an arbitrarily high rental."[21]

In the stipulation of settlement, Tams denied all wrongdoing or liability of any kind arising out of or relating to the claims asserted in the class action and the plaintiffs denied any and all wrongdoing or liability of any kind arising out of claims asserted in Tams' counterclaim and cross-claims.

The stipulation defined "Class Members" as all owners and operators of dinner theaters, musical theaters, playhouses and others who obtained from Tams between June 24, 1972 and September 29, 1976, stage performance rights to musical plays for presentation by substantially professional casts before paying audiences and who were party to or otherwise covered by a contract with Actors Equity Association at the time of at least some of the performances.

Tams first agreed to limit the number of plays which it could acquire during a designated period of time for the purpose of licensing stock stage performance rights to Class Members provided that this restriction did not apply to any plays which are revivals or adaptations of plays as to which Tams then had licensing rights.

In regard to agreements licensing stock performances of plays ("Stock License Agreement") entered into or to be entered into by Class Members, Tams agreed that:

1. It will not increase the rental charges for scores, scripts, vocal and orchestral parts and other like materials and the standard period of rental to any Class Member above those made to such Class Member in the most recent Stock License Agreement with such Class Member for three years except that Tams may increase such charges in any one or more of such three years in accordance with an increase in the consumer price index;

2. Class Members may advertise its licensed engagement immediately after it has executed and returned to Tams by certified mail the Stock License Agreement which was submitted; provided that the licensee shall have returned such Agreement to Tams within two weeks following its receipt thereof and shall have paid to Tams any payment then due under said Agreement;

3. Class Members will not be required by Tams to make any payment called for under a Stock License Agreement by any method of payment other than ordinary check; provided that Tams may require all or some payments to be made by cashier's or certified check if a Class Member presents a check which is subsequently dishonored, or fails to pay in a substantially timely manner under a Stock License Agreement, or otherwise violates a material provision in a Stock License Agreement and fails to cure same promptly after written notice or presents performances of plays controlled by Tams other than pursuant to a valid Stock License Agreement with Tams or is in receivership, bankruptcy or similar proceedings;

4. Advance payments of royalties under a Stock License Agreement need not be made to Tams more than four

weeks prior to the first performance license under that Agreement unless the Class Member requests materials at an earlier date, in which event the advance payment must be made at such earlier date.

5. In those instances in which Stock License Agreements with Class Members (other than dinner theaters) provide for the payment of royalties to Tams based on a percentage of receipts or gross box office receipts, such receipts shall mean gross box office receipts from the sale of tickets (and admissions if there are not tickets) to the play in question (from sales at all locations), provided that Class Members may deduct from receipts (which deductions shall be separately itemized):

   (a) admission taxes or other taxes which are imposed on admissions which are paid or remitted by a Class Member or collected from a theater patron,

   (b) commissions paid by a Class Member to independent contractors in connection with automated ticket sales or remote ticket sales, provided all such commissions do not exceed 10 percent of the ticket price,

   (c) commissions paid by a Class Member to an independent contractor on subscriptions for more than one show (to be fairly allocated), theater parties and group sales, provided such commissions do not exceed 10 percent of the ticket price,

   (d) fees paid to a national credit card company by a Class Member on ticket sales.

The above definition is effective for 15 years. The stipulation provides that a Class Member is not precluded from negotiating for more favorable terms including further exclusions from gross receipts; .

6. Tams will negotiate in good faith with Class Members individually for a particular Stock License Agreement as to the deduction or exclusion from gross receipts of parking fees included in ticket prices;

7. In those instances in which Stock License Agreements with Class Members (other than dinner theaters) provide for payment of royalties to Tams based upon a percentage

of receipts or gross box office receipts, the stipulation is not designed to constitute an agreement as to the inclusion in or exclusion or deduction from, such receipts of any charges (other than for admission) made on a per-ticket basis. This issue is to be determined in accordance with the respective Stock License Agreements to be entered into by Tams and such Class Members. Evidently, the provisions of this paragraph were designed to cover such items as food, beverages, programs and records.

Because so little has been written about the licensing of stock and amateur rights to Broadway plays, the stipulation in the Tams case is quite informative.

FOOTNOTES

1. Chateau de Ville Productions, Inc. v. Tams-Witmark Music Library, Inc., No. 76 Civ. 2788 (S.D.N.Y.).
2. Plaintiffs' Memorandum of Law in Support of Class Action Status (pages 2 and 3).

Chapter Six

Television Views

Developing the Movie of the Week

The emergence of the made for television motion picture as a popular form of television programming has provided an opportunity for the independent television producer to reap the creative and financial rewards which often flow from a successful production. (As used herein, "independent producer" refers to a producer who is not part of or affiliated with a major production company.)

During the initial stages of development, the producer is able to proceed with a relatively small amount of his own capital at risk. Generally, such stages include finding or creating the property; developing the property into a form suitable for presentation to the network; and entering into an agreement with the network for development of the property into a teleplay.

The property upon which the movie is based may be derived from one of a variety of sources; the primary criterion is that the subject be one which the networks feel will appeal to a vast segment of the television audience.

Producers often turn to true stories to provide the basis for movies in the form of so-called "docudramas." As a result of court cases, however, networks and insurance companies have become increasingly concerned about the production of dramatized versions of actual events and have been more insistent that releases be obtained from each individual who will be depicted in the production. Denoting a person or a work as "fictional" does not necessarily avoid the need for releases because of the holding in the *Bindrim* case[1] (see p. 29 for discussion of the *Bindrim* case) that such a reference is not sufficient to avoid a claim for defamation by one who is depicted in a recognizable manner.

Ordinarily, the producer secures the underlying property by entering into an option agreement with the proprietor of the rights. For the payment of a fee, the producer may, during the option period, develop the property by causing a story and/or teleplay to be written. Only if the producer exercises his option to purchase

169

requisite rights in the property will a more substantial purchase price be payable. Such an arrangement enables the producer to determine whether the network will finance a production based upon the property before he must exercise his option.

In the option agreement, the producer will attempt to acquire, not only the rights to produce a made for television motion picture, but also the rights to produce remakes and sequels thereof, one or more television series based thereon, merchandising rights relating thereto, rights to produce one or more novelizations of the teleplay and such other ancillary rights as may be available.

The independent producer is exposed to financial risk when he acquires the option to the extent of the option price which he pays and the fees of his attorney for preparing the requisite agreements. Only if a development deal is made with a network will the independent producer be reimbursed for the former expenses; rarely will he be reimbursed for the latter unless the picture is produced.

Under the development agreement the network also will reimburse the producer for amounts expended for the services of a mutually agreed upon writer to prepare a story and/or teleplay based upon the property. Within a specified period following delivery of the final draft teleplay, the network must elect whether or not to cause the producer to proceed with the production of the motion picture. If the network elects not to proceed, the producer may then attempt to sell his rights to another network or a third party, subject to the repayment to the network of any sums theretofore expended by it in connection with the development of the property.

In many instances, the initial agreement between the producer and the network will leave for further negotiation the issue of the amount of the license fee payable by the network if it elects to proceed with the production of the motion picture. If the parties are not able to agree, the producer will be prohibited for a period of time (usually one or two years) from licensing the property and teleplay elsewhere.

There are strong incentives for both parties to reach an agreement relating to the license fee. The network, of course, will not wish to see its expenditure of between $30,000 and $100,000 (reimbursement for the option fee, payments to the writer(s) of the teleplay and sometimes payment of a script supervisory fee to the producer) be wasted. The producer, in addition to achieving creative fulfillment, wishes to be paid for his expenditure of time and reap the potentially significant financial rewards attendant to the production of a television movie.

These rewards exist because the typical agreement between the producer and the network provides that in return for a specified license fee (generally between two and three million dollars for a two hour movie) the network will be entitled to make two broadcasts during a specified license period (customarily four years). Although the producer may not, during this period, telecast the production or utilize elements in the underlying property in the United States and certain other areas, the producer, rather than the network, owns the production and all underlying rights. The primary right acquired by the network is to make the broadcasts referred to above.

Accordingly, the independent producer derives benefits in several ways.

First the producer may receive a fee for his services from the budget of the picture.

Second, if the picture is produced for less than the license fee, the producer may retain the amount of the savings. (This situation differs from the production of a pilot for a series, in which case the producer typically is reimbursed only for his actual expenses up to a specified maximum amount.) It has become increasingly difficult for a producer to complete the production for less than the license fee, and the typical producer is compelled to rely on other benefits for its financial rewards.

Third, many motion pictures produced for television may be distributed on a television market by market basis in the United States after the term of the network license period has expired and for television broadcast outside the United States at any time. Occasionally, a motion picture has sufficient appeal to audiences to enable it to be licensed for theatrical exhibition in foreign markets.

For the rights to exploit the motion picture in the above markets, and by other non-broadcast methods, a distributor often will make an advance or guaranteed payment to the producer of the motion picture to be applied against the producer's entitlement to a specified percentage of the proceeds derived by the distributor from the exploitation of the motion picture.

Fourth, and of much significance, is the investment tax credit allocable to the picture. Referred to as "The Only Game In Town"[2] in regard to motion pictures, the investment tax credit may be available to the producer under the appropriate circumstances.

However, the independent producer who does not possess or have access to considerable financial resources frequently will not be able to obtain the benefits of the investment tax credit, even if the network orders the production of a picture; for, it is the policy of the networks to require that any entity to which it makes available production funds be "financially responsible" as determined by the network. Most independent producers, not being "financially responsible" by network standards, are compelled, when production of a picture is ordered, to enter into an agreement with a deficit financier (usually a major production company) and to receive from such entity only a production fee and a percentage of the profits derived from the exploitation of the picture. However, with proper tax planning and cooperation from the potential off-network distributor of the picture, the independent producer in some instances may be able to structure his agreements in a manner which satisfies the network's concern regarding financial responsibility and which allows him to obtain the benefits of the investment tax credit.

FOOTNOTES

1.   Bindrim v. Mitchell, 92 Cal. App. 3d 61, 155 Cal. Rptr. 29, *cert. denied,* 444 U.S. 984 (1979).

2.   "The Investment Tax Credit In Connection With Record Masters and Motion Pictures - The Only Game In Town," Harley Williams, Southern California Law Review (Vol. 52:11, 1979).

First Negotiation and Refusal Clauses in Personal Service Contracts

A lawsuit brought by ABC against sportscaster Warner Wolf, and CBS, Inc. provides "an interesting insight into the fierce competition in the television industry for popular performers and favorable ratings."[1]

In issue was a contractual clause requiring Wolf to negotiate in good faith with his employer, ABC, for the 90 day period from December 6, 1979, through March 4, 1980. For the period of December 6, 1979 through January 19, 1980, negotiation with ABC was to be exclusive. Following March 5, 1980 Wolf was required, before accepting any other offer, to afford ABC a right of first refusal. He could comply with this provision either by refraining from accepting another offer or by first tendering the offer to ABC. The first refusal period expired on June 3, 1980.

The case arose because on February 4, 1980, Wolf signed two agreements with CBS. One was an agreement, effective March 6, 1980, under which Wolf was to render services as a producer of sports specials; the other was an agreement granting Wolf the option, exercisable by Wolf until June 4, 1980, to render services as a sportscaster.

The opinion of the Appellate Division was that Wolf breached both the good faith negotiation and the first refusal provisions of the contract, but that equitable intervention was not warranted.

The Court of Appeals agreed that Wolf had breached his obligation to negotiate in good faith with ABC, but found no basis in the record for the conclusion of the Appellate Division that Wolf violated the first refusal provision.

In regard to the good faith negotiation provision, the Court found that when Wolf signed the production agreement with CBS on February 4, 1980 he obligated himself to refrain from rendering services of any nature to any person, firm or corporation on and after March 6, 1980 and, thus, beginning on February 4, 1980, Wolf

173

was unable, because of this prohibition, to extend his contract with ABC. Accordingly, any negotiations he engaged in with ABC after February 4, without the consent of CBS, were meaningless and could not have been in good faith.

The Court concluded that Wolf had not violated the first refusal provision of his agreement with ABC by entering into the sportcasting contract with CBS on February 4 because the right of first refusal did not apply to offers accepted by Wolf *prior* to the March 5 termination of the ABC agreement. The Court noted that "Wolf could not have breached the right of first refusal by accepting an offer during the term of his employment with ABC."[2] Further, the agreement between Wolf and CBS regarding his services as a sportscaster was tailored carefully in the form of an option which was not exercised until after the expiration of the first refusal period.

In considering whether the breach by Wolf of the good-faith negotiation clause entitled ABC to injunctive relief that would bar Wolf from continued employment at CBS, the Court stated that courts of equity historically have refused to order an individual to perform a contract for personal services. In a footnote, a traditional rationale for refusing affirmative enforcement of a personal service contract is set forth:

"I am not aware that any officer of this Court has that perfect knowledge of the Italian language, or possesses that exquisite sensibility in the auricular nerve which is necessary to understand, and to enjoy with a proper zest, the peculiar beauties of the Italian opera, so fascinating to the fashionable world. There might be some difficulty, therefore, even if the defendant was compelled to sing under the direction and in the presence of a master in chancery, in ascertaining whether he performed his engagement according to its spirit and intent. It would also be very difficult for the master to determine what effect coercion might produce upon the defendant's singing, especially in the livelier arias; although the fear of imprisonment would unquestionably deepen his seriousness in the graver parts of the drama. But one thing at least is certain; his songs will be neither comic, or even semi-serious, while he remains confined in that dismal cage, the debtor's prison of New York."[3]

Adding to this rationale, is the strong suggestion that judicial compulsion of personal services might violate the prohibition of the Thirteenth Amendment against involuntary servitude.

The Court then discussed the concept of "negative enforcement" for a failure to perform an employment agreement. When an employee refuses to render services to an employer in violation of an existing contract, and the services are unique or extraordinary, an injunction may issue in certain circumstances to prevent the employee from furnishing those services to another person for the duration of the contract. Cases have indicated that such an injunction will be warranted if there is an express or clearly implied agreement not to work elsewhere for the period of the contract and if the services are unique.

Once the personal service contract terminates, the possibility of equitable relief against the former employee diminishes appreciably. Only if the employee has expressly agreed not to compete with the employer following the term of the contract, or is threatening to disclose trade secrets or commit another tortious act, will injunctive relief generally be available to the employer. Anticompetitive covenants have been vigorously examined and, as noted in the opinion, no New York case has been found where enforcement of an employee's anticompetitive covenant has been granted following termination of the employment contract solely on the basis of the uniqueness of services.

The rationale for the above approach is the general public policy favoring robust and uninhibited competition and the "powerful considerations of public policy which militate against sanctioning the loss of a man's livelihood."[4]

The Court summarized its position by stating: "Specific enforcement of personal service contracts thus turns initially upon whether the term of employment has expired. If the employee refuses to perform during the period of employment, was furnishing unique services, has expressly or by clear implication agreed not to compete for the duration of the contract and the employer is exposed to irreparable injury, it may be appropriate to restrain the employee from competing until the agreement expires. Once the employment contract has terminated, by contrast, equitable relief is potentially available only to prevent injury from unfair competition or similar tortious behavior or to enforce an express and valid anticompetitive covenant. In the absence of such circumstances, the general policy of unfettered competition should prevail."[5]

Using the above principles in its decision to deny ABC's request for injunctive relief, the Court noted: (a) there was no existing employment agreement between the parties, the original contract having terminated in March, 1980; (b) there was no express anti-competitive covenant that Wolf was violating; and (c) there was no claim of special injury from tortious conduct such as exploitation of trade secrets.

In the opinion of the Court, the breach by Wolf of a general contract negotiation clause, acknowledged to be a serious breach and possibly causing ABC to lose a competitive edge, was not of sufficient gravity to interfere with an individual's livelihood, inhibit free competition, nor to override public policy "which favors the free exchange of goods and services through established market mechanisms."[6]

Anticipating the question of whether its decision would have been different had the Court concluded that Wolf breached the first refusal provision of his contract with ABC, the Court indicated in a footnote that, outside of the personal service area, relief might be obtainable. However, when personal services are involved, such relief would result in an affirmative injunction ordering the employee to perform services for the plaintiff. "Such relief, as discussed, cannot be granted."[7]

The decision specifically was without prejudice to ABC's rights to pursue relief in the form of monetary damages.

In his dissent, Justice Fuchsberg indicated that he would have molded an equitable decree, although one more limited than that which plaintiff proposed. He would have enjoined Wolf from broadcasting for a three month period on the ground that there was in the agreement between Wolf and ABC an express three month negative covenant which, because of Wolf's misconduct, ABC was effectively denied the opportunity to exercise. The dissent takes note of the letter executed between Wolf and ABC in February of 1980 in which Wolf's employment was extended during the ninety day period following termination of the original agreement. Had ABC been aware that Wolf already had committed himself to an exclusivity provision in a producer's contract at this time, had it been aware "of this gross breach, had it not been duped into giving an uninformed consent, it would not have agreed to serve as a self-destructive vehicle for the further enhancement of Wolf's potential for taking his ABC-earned following with him."[8]

The dissent also commented on the majority's insistence that Wolf did not breach the first refusal clause. Referring to the CBS-Wolf option contract, which permitted Wolf to accept formally the CBS sportscasting offer at the end of the first refusal period, as "nothing but a charade," the dissent also took issue with the majority's premise that Wolf could not have breached the first refusal clause when he accepted the producer's agreement during the term of his ABC contract when such agreement contained an exclusivity provision. Such a reading of the arrangement with ABC "frustrates the very purpose for which it had to have been made" and exalts form over substance.

The opinion of the Court of Appeals is useful in setting forth guidelines regarding the enforceability of first negotiation and first refusal clauses in personal service agreements and presents a challenge to draftsmen who represent employers of on-air personalities whose services are considered unique.

FOOTNOTES

1.   American Broadcasting Co. v. Wolf, 430 N.Y.S.2d 275, 76 A.D.2d, *app. dismd.*, 51 N.Y.2d 835, 433 N.Y.S.2d 759, (1980), *aff'd*, 52 N.Y.2d 394, 438 N.Y.S.2d 4:2 (1981).

2.   *Id.* at 6.

3.   *Id.* at 7, n. 4.

4.   *Id.* at 10.

5.   *Id.* at 10.

6.   *Id.* at 12.

7.   *Id.* at 11, n. 7.

8.   *Id.* Fuchsberg, J., dissenting, at 2.

An Unsigned Agreement Upheld

A Court of Appeals decision has ended a four and one-half year legal journey testing the enforceability of an oral agreement relating to a television actor which included all essential terms but the date for commencement of performance.[1]

In June of 1971, MGM entered into an agreement with the American Broadcasting Company in connection with MGM's production of the "Munich Project" pilot film and series. The terms of that agreement provided generally that: (a) MGM was to deliver to ABC on or before August 15, 1971 a script for a two hour pilot film; (b) upon delivery, ABC had an exclusive option to require MGM to deliver a pilot film based upon said script; (c) ABC also had an exclusive option to require MGM to produce and deliver to it programs for a television series based upon said pilot, which series was to commence broadcasting in September or October, 1972 ("fall start") or January or February, 1983 ("midseason start"); (d) if ABC elected a fall start, it was required to exercise the series option on or before April 15, 1972 and if ABC elected a midseason start, it was required to exercise its series option on or before November 12, 1972.

After MGM delivered to ABC the script for the pilot film, ABC exercised its option to require MGM to produce and deliver the "Munich Project" pilot film.

Shortly afterwards, in September of 1971, negotiations were commenced among representatives of MGM, ABC, Roy Scheider and his agent relating to the rendition of acting services by Scheider in the pilot and, if one were ordered, the series. At the time of these negotiations Scheider was a relatively unknown actor, having recently appeared in a minor role in the motion picture "Klute" and in a supporting role in a then unreleased film "The French Connection." For this latter role, Scheider was later nominated for an Academy Award as Best Supporting Actor.

179

On September 30, 1971, it was agreed by representatives of MGM and Scheider that: (a) Scheider would appear in and be paid $20,000 for making the pilot film; (b) Scheider would be paid for any series which resulted from the pilot $5,000 per episode in the first year and escalations of the per episode price in each of four subsequent years; and (c) if a pilot film resulted in a series, MGM would have a one year option from the date of completion of the pilot to utilize Scheider's services in such series. Left unresolved at this time was the billing to be afforded Scheider, but within a few days thereafter, partially on the basis of screenings of "The French Connection" held for executives of MGM and ABC, it was agreed that Scheider would have second star billing in the pilot and first star billing in the series, if any.

Scheider proceeded to Munich, Germany on or about October 6, 1971 where, during a six week period the pilot was shot.

From October, 1971 to mid-February, 1972 MGM's and Scheider's attorneys negotiated the remaining open points of the agreement. During this period MGM submitted a proposed written agreement to which Scheider's attorney responded with his comments. The trial court later found that by February 15, 1972 all but one of the proposed terms had been agreed upon in substance, although the language of some of the provisions remained to be drafted. The point not agreed upon was the date on which Scheider would be required to report to start filming the series, were one ordered. At the trial, there was conflicting testimony concerning this point. Scheider's attorney testified that his understanding of the agreement was that Scheider would not be required to report for the commencement of principal photography of a series earlier than November 1, 1972. He acknowledged that such limitation would make impossible the commencement of broadcasting of the series in the fall of 1972. MGM's attorneys denied that this limitation was contained in the parties' agreement and contended that Scheider contrived the dispute as to his reporting date in order to avoid his contractual commitment to MGM.

In November of 1971, after Scheider had returned from filming the pilot in Munich, he met with William Friedkin who was planning the production of "The Exorcist" and Scheider discussed with him the possibility of playing the male lead in that film. MGM eventually alleged that "the subsequent 'misunderstanding' which arose with respect to a start date for the series can be fully explained by Scheider's desire to accept the role in 'The Exorcist.'"[2]

In April of 1972, ABC exercised its option to require MGM to produce and deliver eight episodes of the series (the name having been changed to "Assignment in Vienna") for a fall start, and MGM thereafter exercised its option requiring Scheider to report on or before June 5, 1972 for filming of the series. Scheider refused. MGM then brought an action in Supreme Court, New York County seeking damages and to enjoin Scheider from entering into an agreement which would require him to perform services which would conflict with those he was obligated to render for MGM. The non-jury trial commenced April 24, 1972.

The Court determined the issue to be whether the terms which were agreed upon by the parties were sufficient to support a finding that the parties had made an agreement, and if so, whether that agreement was enforceable under the Statute of Frauds. The latter issue will not be treated in this discussion.

In finding that a complete contract did exist, the Court first noted that many of the basic elements of the contract were left for future negotiations at the time of the September 30, 1971 understanding, but then stated:

"However, where the parties have completed their negotiations of what they regard as essential elements, and performance has begun on the good faith understanding that agreement on the unsettled matters will follow, the court will find and enforce a contract even though the parties have expressly left these other elements for further negotiation and agreement, if some objective method of determination is available, independent of either party's mere wish or desire. Such objective criteria may be found in the agreement itself, commercial practice or other usage and custom. If the contract can be rendered certain and complete, by reference to something certain, the court will fill in the gaps. Here, the subsequent agreement of the parties as to all the elements of the contract, except the starting date, provides a basis for finding a complete contract."[3]

In disposing of the unresolved issue as to the start date for the filming of the series the Court cited the testimony at the trial pertaining to the custom and practice of the industry in this regard and found it to be undisputed that all of the parties were aware of these customs and practices and that the agreement between ABC and MGM was consistent therewith.

The Court concluded: "Enough has been shown as to the customs and practice of the industry, the understanding of the parties, and their subsequent agreement as to terms, to establish a contract requiring Scheider to report during the spring of 1972 for a September, 1972 air date, if so requested by MGM. This is a reasonable time which may be implied by law, even if not agreed upon."[4]

Having concluded that an agreement existed, the Court then held that said agreement was unenforceable because it violated the Statute of Frauds, because by its terms it was not to be performed within one year from the making thereof.

On appeal, the Appellate Division unanimously modified the lower court judgment on the law to dismiss the defense of Statute of Frauds. It reinstated the complaint, granted injunctive relief sought by MGM and remanded the case to Trial Term for an assessment of damages occasioned by defendant's breach of contract.[5] The findings of fact made at the non-jury trial were approved and adopted by the Appellate Division.

The decision of Judge Carney who tried the issue of damages noted that ABC, having already obtained a sponsor and committed itself to show the episodes, insisted that Robert Conrad take the place of Scheider. Conrad, being aware that Scheider was refusing to complete the contract, was in a position virtually to dictate the terms of his contract.

For each of the eight episodes which were produced, Conrad received the sum of $17,500 plus certain additional payments, all totaling $183,488. This amount was $120,888 more than MGM would have been required to pay to Scheider under his contract had he performed in the same eight episodes, and this amount was awarded by the Court as damages to MGM, with interest.

The Court of Appeals wrote the final chapter of this journey in its decision which stated that the findings of fact by the Court at the first trial were beyond the scope of its review, noted that the defense based on the Statute of Frauds had been abandoned on appeal and found without merit Scheider's objection to the Appellate Division's remand for a second trial on the issue of damages. It then affirmed the decision of Justice Carney.

The four volume Record of Appeal of this case is interesting reading for anyone involved in the television industry, not only because of the legal issues involved, but also because of the detailed testimony presented by each party relating to the negotiation of Scheider's employment contract.

FOOTNOTES

1. Metro-Goldwyn-Mayer, Inc. v. Scheider, 40 NY2d 1069, 392 N.Y.S.2d 252 (1976).
2. *Id.* Brief for Plaintiff-Respondent at 5.
3. 75 Misc.2d 422.
4. *Id.* at 423.
5. 43 A.D.2d 922.

Renegotiating Television Agreements

An article by attorney and television producer Larry A. Thompson sets forth a proposal designed to eliminate the need for renegotiating agreements with producers and actors relating to a successful prime time television series.[1] The article is of interest, not only because of Thompson's concepts, but also because of the knowledge it imparts regarding the television industry.

Thompson begins by citing contractual demands made by several television stars which, on first impression, appear outrageous, and then postulates that the inherent problem rests with the contractual relationships which exist between performer and producer, on the one hand, and the producer and television network, on the other.

At the point in the typical step deal between the producer as supplier and owner of the programs and the network as licensee when the teleplay has been prepared and the network has requested that a pilot be produced, Thompson notes that the producer has his choice of literally thousands of eager actors. He may then engage several actors to test for parts in the pilot (with the usual requirement that the network has final approval over who is chosen). It is at this stage, even before the test occurs, that the performer may enter into an agreement with the producer in which the producer is granted the option to engage the services of the performer for an initial period of time and for options thereafter which often total between five and seven years. The performer is paid a specific fee for each episode in which he appears, and frequently is guaranteed payment for appearances in a specific minimum number of episodes per year. The fee will escalate by a predetermined amount (often 10 percent cumulatively) for each year in which the producer exercises its option. Unless the performer is in particular demand, he receives neither a percentage of the profits of the program nor contingent payments tied into the success of the series. The agreement normally contains no prohibition against the producer's terminating the services of the actor if the series is cancelled or if the producer elects to do so for any other reason.

185

The above agreement roughly parallels the one between the producer and the network. Under that license agreement, the network orders a specific number of programs from the producer during each year (with an option for the network to increase the number of programs so ordered in a given year), and has options to order programs in subsequent years. The license fee paid to the producer for each episode is designed to cover all costs incurred by the producer in the production of that episode. This fee, like that of the performer, increases on a year-to-year basis.

Unlike the performer, the producer is exposed to an out-of-pocket loss in connection with the production of episodes of the series; for, it is not unusual that the costs of producing the episodes exceed the license fee from the network. This deficit financing is borne by the producer in the hope that a successful series will develop and that the off-network syndication sale of the series will result in large profits. Often, the producer will elect to spend more money on the production of the programs, thereby increasing his cash flow deficit, in order to produce a better product and one more likely to be sold in the syndicated market. It is customary that for a program to have any real value for domestic syndication, at least 66 programs must have been produced.

Under such circumstances, it is difficult for a producer to accede to a star performer's demand to renegotiate his contract, especially in the early years of the series when a successful syndicated sale is not yet guaranteed. Thus, when the performer requests additional compensation from the producer, the producer often will ask that the network pay or reimburse the additional amount. Because of the enormous profits which a network typically generates from a successful series, it is not unusual that the network complies with this request.

Under this scenario, "a hit TV series licensing fee and its stars' salaries are the heated focal points of constant renegotiations. It is a literal free-for-all with the network keeping its books closed, the producer calming his nervous banker, and the Star moaning about his injured back and unable to work."[2]

According to Thompson, creative contract structuring at the beginning of the relationship among the parties would anticipate and provide contingencies in the case of future failures or successes. The proposed structure would balance the leverage maintained by the producer and the network at the outset of the negotiations and that held by the star as the series becomes recognized as a success.

In presenting his position, Thompson maintains that television is the only entertainment-oriented business which does not provide a success clause for its talent.

He states that the recording artist and the songwriter each are paid on the basis of every record sold and every record manufactured respectively and, thus, the more records which are manufactured and sold, the more money the recording artist and songwriter make. (Given the significant number of renegotiations which occur in the recording industry with respect to recording artists who achieve success, this built-in success formula frequently is ineffective.)

Book publishers pay authors a royalty on the basis of each book sold, promoters of concerts pay the artist a guaranteed fee per performance plus a percentage of the gate over a specified amount, and motion picture stars traditionally have received a percentage of the profits of the films in which they appear. (Much has been written, however, about the dissatisfaction of those who share in net profits because of the manner in which same are defined and computed.)

The structure which Thompson suggests mandates the payment to the producer of an amount, in addition to the licensing fee payable per episode, calculated by using a formula based on the ratings success of the program, and requires that this extra amount be divided between the producer and the regular cast of the programs on a pre-set sliding scale basis. To help understand the proposal, an analysis of the Nielsen Rating System (conducted since 1950 by the A.C. Nielsen Company) is presented.

Nielsen samples approximately 1,250 homes to project what programs the estimated 217 million people in the 82 million U.S. television households are watching.

"Each night Nielsen projects the percentage of homes actually 'using' television (HUT) and the percentage (or Share) of those homes which are watching any 'given program' at any given time. The multiplication of the Share Percentage times the HUT Percentage equals the Rating Percentage. The Rating Percentage multiplied by the total number of possible 'TV households' is the number of 'homes watching that particular program.' The number of 'homes'

watching that particular program times the available audience viewers per home of 2.6 is the number of 'people' watching that particular
program."[3]

Advertisers pay advertising rates based upon the cost per thousand of homes reached by a program. According to Thompson, the
average licensing fee paid by the network to a producer for a one
hour prime time television program is $650,000 for two runs, and
the average fee for a 30 minute program is $350,000 for two runs.

Using the foregoing information, one may compute the gross
advertising receipts derived by the network for a particular program,
the total cost to the network for licensing that program and the
gross profit to the network of that program. As an example, Thompson cites the program "Magnum, P.I." which last season had a
rating of 20.8 for the first run and rerun of each episode. Assuming
a 65 percent HUT, a cost to the advertiser of $5.50 per thousand
homes reached and 22 original programs and 22 reruns, the network
would have grossed $49,228,608. Further, assuming a license fee of
$650,000 for 22 first run and repeat programs, the total cost to the
network would have been $14.3 million. The network's gross profit
for the year would be $34,928,608 for this program.

Thompson proposes that the additional amount referred to above
to be divided between the producer and the cast (designated as the
Additional Income Differential ["AID"]) be calculated by deducting
from the yearly gross income of of a program ("PYGI") the yearly
projected income of the program ("PYPI"). The latter amount
"would be tied to a base rating equal to the seasonal average rating
achieved by the industry average comparable program as reported
by Nielsen for the full TV season immediately preceding the commencement of the contract"[4] plus a return on investment to the
network which would take into consideration the network's high
overhead, expense of development costs and losses on unsuccessful
shows.

As the show remains on the air and the ratings escalate, the
network will increase its price to the advertiser thus increasing the
PYGI and the AID. (Thompson notes that networks do not simply
bill an advertiser for the actual number of viewers reached, but
rather enters into a contract prior to broadcast at the going market
value based on a projected audience profile rating.) The AID would
be paid to the producer at the end of each 52-week period. If, during

any period the network's **PYGI** is less than the amount projected, the network would be entitled to recoup from the producer's future annual bonus, if any, the amount of the deficiency. This deficiency may be carried forward, but not backward.

Because the producer bears the risk of loss until approximately the third season of program production, Thompson proposes that the **AID** be shared between the producer and the regular cast of the show in the following proportions: year one, 60 percent to producer and 40 percent to cast; year two, 50 percent to producer and 50 percent to cast; year three, 40 percent to producer and 60 percent to cast; year four, 30 percent to producer and 70 percent to cast; year five, 20 percent to producer and 80 percent to cast; year six, 10 percent to producer and 90 percent to cast; and year seven, no percent to producer and 100 percent to cast. The rationale behind this scale is that the talent should receive increasing participations in later years, because they usually own no portion of the programs and will not share in the producer's syndicated profits which become more of a reality the longer the series is telecast.

Thompson proposes that a ten point system be used to determine the manner in which the cast of the series shares among themselves the percentage of the **AID**. The sole star of the series would be entitled to more points than co-stars or tri-leads. Thompson acknowledges that the contract formula cannot provide for every contingency, and cites the problem which will occur if the contracted fourth lead of the series suddenly "takes off" and substantially overshadows the leads, as well as adding additional ratings to the program. No mention is made of if and how the number of points allocated to a particular cast member should be affected if that person shares in the profits of the series nor the affect on the morale and cohesiveness of the cast if the performers are negotiating against one another for a greater share of available points.

It is apparent that the constant threat of and request for renegotiation among performers, producers and networks leads to unhealthy friction which diminishes the creative process and often adversely affects the programs in question. Besides presenting a proposal which provides an informed basis for discussion regarding a creative solution to a difficult problem, Thompson's article is filled with interesting information and useful facts for anybody involved in the television industry.

FOOTNOTES

1. Larry A. Thompson, "The Prime Time Crime," 1 *Entertainment Law Journal* 1 (3rd issue, 1982).
2. *Id.*
3. *Id.*
4. *Id.*

Fourth Networks

"The 'fourth network' is inevitable. It's just a question of when, and that depends on the advertisers."[1] This recent quote from a television executive is made at a time when advertising agencies, program suppliers and broadcasters are intensifying their efforts to create alternatives to purchasing advertising time and presenting programs on the three free commercial television networks, ABC, NBC and CBS.

These networks dominate the television industry. In addition to the stations which it owns and operates, each network is affiliated with hundreds of local stations to which it makes cash payments and supplies programming. The affiliate has the option, but not the obligation, to broadcast these programs. The network sells commercial minutes in each program to national advertisers and, in regard to some programs (such as the "Today" and "Tonight" shows), the affiliate may sell commercial time to local advertisers.

There is little consistency in the use of the term "fourth network." At times the words refer to programs produced for first-run syndication, yet syndicating a television program is different from exhibiting a program on a network.

Also, both "Operation Prime Time" ("OPT") and the "Nixon Interviews with David Frost" were described as having been distributed by fourth networks, although the financing and marketing of the programs differed markedly. The former, an enterprise which supplies four to ten hours of programming each year, made its debut several years ago with six hours of programming based on Taylor Caldwell's novel *Testimony of Two Men.* The production was broadcast on over 90 stations, which sold the bulk of advertising time locally and held back only two minutes of commercial time for sale nationally by OPT. The latter was financed with monies obtained from private sources. The completed programs then were given free of charge to the stations comprising the network, with approximately

191

five minutes of national advertising time already contained in each program. The revenue from the sale of this time was used to reimburse the production costs for the programs. The stations broadcasting the programs were able to sell approximately seven minutes of advertising time in each program to local advertisers.

References to fourth networks, however, consistently do refer to an authentic free commercial television alternative to ABC, NBC and CBS which utilizes national advertising on some basis.

The relationship between programming and advertising is explained in part in an analysis by Les Brown, the respected television columnist. In his book *Television, The Business Behind the Box,* Brown wrote:

". . . the Nielsen numbers are the real product of American television. They are what the networks sell to advertisers and what the programs are designed for. A show has a 20.0 rating at 8:30 at night. That is 12 million television homes, or 25,250,000 people, and Nielsen breaks that figure down to young, old and in between. This is what the advertiser buys, the numbers and the breakdown; conceivably, he may never learn the name of the show.

"The game of television is basically between the network and the advertiser, and the Nielsen digits determine what the latter will pay for the circulation of his commercial. The public is involved only as the definition of the number: so many persons 18 to 49, so many others, all neatly processed by television.

"In day-to-day commerce, television is not so much interested in the business of communications as in the business of delivering people to advertisers. People are the merchandise, not the shows. The shows are merely the bait."[2]

The interest of advertisers in fourth networks is evidenced by their involvement in several new plans.

McCann-Erickson, Inc. intends to establish an ad hoc movie network to broadcast feature films after they have been released on pay television, but before they have been broadcast on network television.

Lexington Broadcasting Services, a successful seller of barter time in syndication, expects to sell during the next broadcast season $120 million of national-bartered time in at least 21 syndicated programs. The chairman of this company contends that "this enormous volume makes LBS a legitimate fourth network because the spots are studded throughout the entire broadcast day in a wide variety of programs,"[3] including "Fame" and "Too Close For Comfort" (both being sold in first-run syndication after having been cancelled by the networks), and several off-network syndicated series. In regard to "Fame," Lexington has agreed to guarantee to the distributor several million dollars in return for the right to sell five national minutes of advertising time in each episode.

Program suppliers, in addition to the producers of "Fame" and "Too Close For Comfort," have announced interest in the fourth network concept. Paramount Television will introduce a first-run weekly series to be delivered by satellite to in excess of 100 stations. Embassy Television has expressed its intention to create a fourth network for the purpose of licensing feature films which have been sold on pay television but not on the three television networks.

Broadcasters with the stated purpose of gaining "a better foothold on software for our stations"[4] also are anxious to explore the possibilities of a fourth network. Tribune Company Broadcasting Inc., Taft Broadcasting Co., Gaylord Broadcasting Co. and Chris Craft Industries Inc. have formed a joint venture to create a network that will offer once a week in prime time advertiser supported films and perhaps, eventually, made for television films. When implemented, this network will start with a base of 15 independent stations owned by the four companies covering 36 percent of the United States television homes.

Also, Metromedia is in the process of establishing a fourth network of independent stations, which will begin by presenting feature films once a month and later, if possible, proceed to once-a-week presentations.

To help implement this plan, Metromedia has entered into an agreement with Home Box Office for distribution on its commercial network of movies made for pay television. Under the arrangement, Metromedia will have the right for two years to broadcast on its network eight films initially made for and transmitted on HBO, and will also have the right to distribute said movies in worldwide syndication at a time following its broadcast of the movies. As part of the arrangement, Metromedia has agreed to provide financing for motion pictures which are made in the first instance for HBO.

The emergence of fourth networks will require representatives to focus on several issues. For example, talent which is entitled to receive a royalty for each new episode of a television series which is produced must be certain that the royalty is payable regardless of whether the program is produced for one of the three television networks or for any other network-type operation. In this regard, it may be appropriate to adjust the royalty if the program is not produced for either ABC, NBC or CBS.

Also, in certain instances, special arrangements may have to be made with the unions. The producers of "Fame," for instance, are reported to have made an arrangement with Screen Actors Guild which allows a second broadcast of each program to be made in non-prime time during the same week in which the first broadcast was made.

Finally, agreements involving advertising agencies will be complex, requiring that issues be covered such as what occurs if the audience delivered does not meet up to expectations.

Fourth networks represent a further challenge to the dominance of the three networks, which already face growing competition from cable and pay television. If they are successful, the impact on the advertising and broadcasting industries will be significant.

FOOTNOTES

1. *Broadcasting*, July 4, 1983, Page 70, quoting John E. Goldhammer, Senior Vice President for Programming, Paramount Television.

2. At pages 15 and 16.

3. *Variety*, June 29, 1983, Page 33.

4. *Broadcasting*, February 14, 1983, Page 36, quoting James C. Dowdle, President of Tribune Company Broadcasting.

The Substantial Impact of Pay Television

New technologies, and pay television in particular, have had substantial affects on motion picture financing and exploitation.

First, pay-television has provided a substantial outlet for the sale of ancillary rights in motion pictures. The increase in available revenues has allowed more leeway for the expenditure of larger amounts on production budgets.

A second effect, related to the first, has been to raise the value of studios' film libraries. For example, the approximately 4,400 films estimated to be in the MGM/UA library (the biggest of the major Hollywood studios) has been estimated to have a value of in excess of $675 million; this film library has been described in a report as "a perpetual annuity."

Third, the release pattern of the typical motion picture has changed. Today, the initial release for a film generally is more widespread and intense than in the past in order to enable the distributor to maximize film rentals as quickly as possible prior to the exploitation of the picture in ancillary markets.

Fourth, the appetite of the free television networks for films previously shown on pay television has diminished, and in those instances when the networks are willing to purchase such pictures they are not willing to pay the same amounts as they once were. A motion picture exhibited on pay television, a medium which has a rapidly growing subscriber base, possibly will not be watched during its network runs by many of those who previously have seen the film. This, in turn, will affect the network's ratings and the amount of money that the network can charge its advertisers.

Various reports, as well as papers filed with the Federal Communications Commission, indicate that the total audience watching the networks has diminished in recent years. For example, statistics submitted by the American Broadcasting Company indicate that the average prime time audience drawn by the three television net-

195

works has dropped despite increased growth in the number of television sets.

A fifth effect has been to change the manner in which companies license films to syndicated television. Whereas previously, stations would be offered a six or seven year license term (being allowed as many as ten runs of each movie during that term), now the marketing plans of several companies have changed so that only three or four year license periods are available. The reason for the change is to be able to retrieve the pictures from syndication as quickly as possible in order to sell them again to cable.

A sixth effect has been to diminish the non-theatrical market (which is the sale or rental of programming to schools, homes, churches, libraries, prisons and similar institutions). With pay television and videocassettes now available to many of these markets, there is less demand for the same product to be made available by the non-theatrical distributor.

Seventh, the pay cable (and basic cable) market has been of great benefit to those companies—in some instances subsidiaries of major distributors—which are engaged in the exploitation of art films and similar "small" pictures. An executive of a major company involved in such exploitation has been quoted as stating: "People think I'm in the art house business. I'm in the cable business. We've been quietly buying pictures that will be quite profitable on cable and videocassettes after they play enough art houses for the word to get around."

Eighth, pay television has been in part responsible for spawning proposed "fourth networks" which, among other activities, may buy theatrical movies that studios have not sold to the networks.

Ninth, in an unlikely analogy to the world of politics strange entertainment bedfellows have been made. In large measure to counter the growing power of Home Box Office ("HBO"), the Showtime and Movie Channel pay systems have become jointly owned by Viacom International, Inc., Warner Communications, Inc., and Warner Amex Cable Communications. Also Columbia Picures, CBS and HBO have formed a joint venture presently known as "Tri-Star," and Columbia Pictures, Orion and The Cannon Group each have entered into separate ventures with HBO.

The tenth effect has been to foster the emergence of the pay-per-view industry. Now in its infancy, this industry is regarded by many executives as having more potential to generate revenue than other forms of motion picture distribution. They point to the time when millions of subscribers around the world each will pay between five and ten dollars to watch a particular event.

As the number of subscribers able to receive pay-per-view programming increases, as the addressable converters necessary to service this enterprise become more sophisticated and as direct broadcast satellites and high definition television become widespread, the predictions of those executives may become a reality.

The effects of pay television outlined above have occurred at a time when the number of subscribers is a fraction of what it ultimately will be. It is likely that as the industry ages its impact on other industries will spread and be even more pronounced.

Summary of Speech for American Bar Association Forum Committee on Entertainment and Sports Industries, March 18, 1983 (published in *New York Law Journal).*

Chapter Seven
Music Matters

The Re-Recording Restriction—"Could It Be Magic"

Most contracts between a recording artist and his record company restrict the artist from recording for others for a period of time any composition which he records during the term of that contract. This re-recording restriction was the basis of a motion involving Barry Manilow's rendition of the composition "Could It Be Magic."

Manilow and Daylight Productions, Inc. had entered into an agreement (the "Recording Agreement") which provided that during its term Manilow would render his recording services exclusively for Daylight. The expressed intention of this Recording Agreement was that Daylight would enter into a contract with a third party distributor to which Daylight would furnish Manilow's services and which would have the right to manufacture and distribute records containing Manilow's performances.

The Recording Agreement provided for a five year re-recording restriction as follows:

"During the term of this agreement, (Manilow) will not perform for the purpose of making phonograph records or master recordings for any person other than (Daylight), and during a period of five years after the expiration of the term of this agreement, for any reason whatsoever, (Manilow) will not perform any musical composition which shall have been recorded hereunder for any person other than (Daylight) for the purpose of making phonograph records or master recordings . . ."

"(Manilow) will not at any time manufacture, distribute or sell or authorize or knowingly permit the manufacture, distribution or sale by any person other than (Daylight) of phonograph records embodying, . . . after the expiration of the term hereof, any performance of a composition recorded hereunder, rendered by (Manilow) prior to the date five (5) years subsequent to the expiration date of the term of this agreement."

"(Manilow) will not record or authorize or knowingly permit to be recorded for any purpose any such performance without in each case taking reasonable measures to prevent the manufacture, distribution and sale at any time by any person other than (Daylight) of phonograph records embodying such performances. Specifically, without limiting the generality of the foregoing, (Manilow) agree(s) that . . . if, after the expiration of the term of this agreement, (Manilow) perform(s) for any such purpose any composition which shall have been recorded pursuant to this agreement, and such performance is rendered by (Manilow) prior to the date five (5) years subsequent to the expiration date of the term of this agreement, (Manilow) will do so only pursuant to a written contract containing an express provision that neither such performance nor any recording therof will be used, directly or indirectly, for the purpose of making phonograph records."

The Recording Agreement also provided that Daylight could assign its rights in the master recordings to a distributor.

A second agreement (the "Production Agreement") was entered into among Thau-Merenstein Productions and Manilow on the one hand and Daylight on the other. Paragraph 2 thereof authorized Thau-Merenstein exclusively during the term to negotiate and execute agreements pursuant to which master recordings recorded under the Recording Agreement would be sold, assigned and transferred to a record distributor. A Rider to the Production Agreement specified:

"Under no circumstances is this agreement to be interpreted as granting Thau-Merenstein the right to the recording services of Manilow except as such services are rendered by Manilow to (Daylight) pursuant to the recording agreement."

The Production Agreement was to terminate if Thau-Merenstein was not able to enter into an agreement with a distributor within 60 days. It neither contained nor referred to a re-recording restriction.

Thau-Merenstein entered into a distribution agreement ("the Distribution Agreement") with Bell Records on February 23, 1971 which provided that Bell would have exclusive and perpetual ownership of master recordings containing Manilow's performances delivered to it thereunder and the absolute right to dispose of and deal in and with the same on any conditions as Bell determined.

The Distribution Agreement also contained warranties and agreements by Thau-Merenstein that:

"Daylight has a valid, existing agreement with (Manilow, and) . . . that said agreement absolutely restricts (Manilow) from recording the compositions embodied upon the Masters for a period of at least five (5) years from the date of recording such composition, . . ." and that ". . . for a period of five (5) consecutive years from the date hereof it will not record or produce nor will it permit others to record or produce phonograph records embodying a performance by (Manilow) of the compositions embodied upon the Masters for anyone other than (Bell)."

Manilow, not a party to the Distribution Agreement, executed a side letter to Bell warranting that he was bound to an exclusive recording agreement with Daylight and agreeing to perform directly for Bell in the event of certain contingencies.

While these three agreements were in effect, and while he was a relatively obscure talent, Manilow recorded "Could It Be Magic." Sales of this recording were small and the various papers filed in connection with the motion referred to the record as a "flop." Subsequently, after plaintiff's contractual relationship with Daylight and Manilow had expired, Manilow re-recorded the song for Arista Records, the successor company to Bell, with resulting sales in excess of $3 million. It is undisputed that the re-recording of the song occurred within the five year restricted period referred to in the Recording Agreement.

Thau-Merenstein then brought suit against Daylight, Manilow and Arista for breach of contract and an accounting for its share of record royalties.[1] Defendant Manilow moved to dismiss the complaint for failure to state a cause of action.

The decision summarized the position of the parties as follows:

"Plaintiff's basic position is that the Production Agreement effectively contains an assignment to itself of Daylight's rights vis-à-vis Manilow under the terms of the five year re-recording restriction, which clause 'is found in every recording contract in the industry.' Plaintiff argues that the Production Agreement and the Recording Agreement are interdependent contracts, and that plaintiff was an intended beneficiary of the Recording Agreement, just as the Production Agreement anticipated and controlled the Distribution Agreement. Plaintiff further maintains that the provisions of paragraph 4(a) of the Recording Agreement (which assigns to Daylight the ownership of all Masters recorded by Manilow) should be read together with the provisions of paragraph 2 of the Production Agreement (which binds Daylight to furnish plaintiff, exclusively, with Manilow's services). In sum, it is plaintiff's contention that the overall import of the Recording Agreement and the Production Agreement compels the construction that Daylight thereby agreed, in the event plaintiff contracted with a recording company on Manilow's behalf, to share with plaintiff Daylight's exclusive right to Manilow's artistic output, including the protection afforded by the re-recording restriction."

"Manilow's position can be briefly stated as follows: The Production Agreement does not incorporate by reference the terms of the Recording Agreement for the purposes asserted by plaintiff, but, on the contrary, merely provides for plaintiff to act as co-producer with Daylight of Manilow's Master Recordings with the right to share with Daylight in the producer's share of royalties."

The Court determined that the Production Agreement contained no language which could be construed as incorporating, in favor of plaintiff, the re-recording restriction contained in the Recording Agreement. The decision stated:

"It would appear that if the parties had intended that the benefits of the re-recording restriction to be extended to plaintiff, at the least, specific mention of this provision would have been made in the Production Agreement."

". . . Indeed, the Distribution Agreement entered into on February 23, 1971, with Bell Records, expressly assigns to the latter the right to enforce against Manilow, the terms of the re-recording restriction. Thus, any question as to whether the Production Agreement conveyed to plaintiff the benefit of this restriction becomes academic in light of the subsequent transfer to Bell Records of such benefit in the Distribution Agreement."

The Court, stating that proof of a general trade custom may not be interposed to vary or contradict unambiguous contractual provisions, also rejected plaintiff's argument that because a re-recording restriction is customarily included in record industry agreements, plaintiff was entitled to the presumption that such was the parties' intention in this instance.

An interesting aspect of this motion, not mentioned in the Court's decision, is that Plaintiff here sought to use the re-recording restriction affirmatively—to obtain a share of royalties from a subsequent version of the composition—rather than negatively—to prevent the artist from diminishing the value of a production previously delivered to the recording company.

FOOTNOTES

1.   Thau-Merenstein Productions, Inc. v. Arista Records, Inc., No. 51504/76 (Sup. Ct. Mar. 16, 1977), *aff'd*, 65 A.D.2d 681, *appeal denied*, 47 N.Y.2d 705.

The Discreet Lawsuit

A letter, similar in form to the following, often is sent by record companies to their competitors when a contractual dispute arises with one of their recording artists:

"Gentlemen:

"This letter is to inform you that (Recording Artist) is signed to an exclusive long term recording agreement with (Recording Company). Any attempts to interfere with (Recording Company's) contractual rights, by any person or firm, will be acted upon immediately and vigorously.

"Please be advised that this same notice is being sent to all active record companies."

A decision reached by a jury in California[1] may cause record companies and their attorneys to evaluate carefully the advisability of sending such letters, especially in a situation when there is a legitimate dispute between the company and the artist.

The case involved a singer professionally known as Kathy Dalton who entered into an Exclusive Recording Artist Agreement with Discreet Records, Inc. That agreement required Dalton to complete at least one album in each 18 month period and granted to Discreet the right to require delivery of one additional album during each such period. The compositions to be recorded by Dalton were to be selected jointly by Dalton and her producers, subject to the approval of Discreet, not to be withheld unreasonably.

The first album produced under the agreement was released in October, 1973. In February, 1974 an executive of Discreet demanded that a second album be recorded, but as later alleged by Dalton, would not allow her to include on that album six compositions previously recorded by her, heard by said executive and considered by him to be satisfactory. Dalton later alleged that Discreet had demanded at the time of such request that she record material not compatible with the style that the public associated with her.

On May 6, 1974 Discreet notified Dalton that because of Dalton's refusal to perform in accordance with her agreement, it was electing to suspend such agreement for a period equal to the period of Dalton's refusal to perform. Dalton responded on May 27, 1974, stating first, that since the said agreement was dated May 18, 1973 she could not be in breach of a provision requiring delivery of a second album during the initial 18 month period thereof until November 18, 1974, and second, that she never stated she would not complete her obligation to record masters for Discreet. Dalton then indicated that a continuation of the suspension would be deemed by her to be a material breach of the agreement. She further stated that Discreet had breached the agreement by unreasonably withholding approval of the six compositions recorded but not released on the first album because, she asserted, the clear understanding of the parties on signing the agreement was that the style of the compositions on the first album would be similar to those on the second.

Discreet responded, reiterating and elaborating upon its position, and Dalton, on June 10, 1974 advised Discreet that because the agreement between them contained a clause requiring any material breach to be cured within thirty days after notice, and because Dalton had notified Discreet of such material breaches by letter dated May 27, 1974, Discreet had until June 26, 1974 to cure such breaches, failing which Dalton would thereafter terminate the agreement.

On June 28, 1974 Dalton wrote to Discreet terminating the agreement and to Warner Bros. Records advising them that she stood ready, willing and able to perform for Warner Bros. under the Artist Inducement Letter which she had previously signed. (Warner Bros., the distributor of the record product of Discreet, required recording artists signed to Discreet to execute such an Inducement Letter stating that if the agreement between the artist and Discreet were terminated, the artist would render services to Warner directly with the same effect as if the artist agreement with Discreet were directly between the artist and Warner). Warner subsequently responded to Dalton's attorney that Warner would not entertain such a direct contractual relationship.

When Discreet offered by letter dated September 3, 1974 to arrange recording dates for Dalton, she responded that the offer was not timely made since the agreement had been terminated effective June 28, 1974. Discreet's attorney then wrote Dalton stating that if she failed to record her next album for Discreet within 120 days, Discreet would seek a court order enjoining Dalton from recording for any other firm and would "inform every major record company that any attempt by them to record (Dalton) will result in an active lawsuit against them for general, specific, and punitive damages for interference with contractual rights."

Shortly after this letter was received, Dalton received a further letter from Discreet purporting to exercise Discreet's option contained in the recording agreement to increase the compensation payable to Dalton to at least $6,000 per year. The bases for this offer were California statutes which provide generally that an injunction may not be granted to prevent the breach of a contract relating to the furnishing of personal services unless the minimum compensation for such services is at the rate of not less than $6,000 per year. Dalton later claimed in her affidavits that at no time prior or subsequent to her receiving this letter did Discreet tender to her sums which would yield compensation of not less than $6,000 per year.

On or about September 19, 1974 Discreet sent out letters to record companies in a form similar to the letter referred to at the beginning of this article. Dalton's attorney, on learning that such letters were sent, wrote Discreet on October 14, 1974 stating that such letters were unprivileged and unlawful interferences with Dalton's contractual rights for which she would hold Discreet fully liable in damages or otherwise.

Dalton then sought to enter into a recording agreement with companies other than Discreet, and on or about March 1, 1975 entered into such an agreement with Island Records, Inc.

Thereafter, Discreet sought a preliminary injunction to prevent Dalton from performing as a recording artist for Island. Because the Court felt that the recording agreement between Dalton and Discreet did not sufficiently comply with the requirements of the California statutes referred to above relating to minimum compensation of $6,000 per year, the Court denied such relief.

Subsequently, Dalton and her producer Greg Dempsey filed a cross-complaint against Discreet which sought, among other rem-

edies, both actual and exemplary damages arising from the interference and related activities of Discreet in regard to Dalton's seeking
a new recording agreement.

After trial, the jury decided to dismiss the complaint of Discreet
and to award Dalton and Dempsey damages totaling $68,000. Sig-
nificantly, $12,000 of this sum was awarded to Dalton as punitive
damages.

Although this case involves an unusual set of facts, attorneys
representing record companies should not dismiss lightly the verdict
in this case when evaluating whether to send and what to include
in notice letters to competitors of their clients.

FOOTNOTES

1. Discreet v. Dalton, No. 122536 (California 1977).

After the Group Disbands

What is the obligation of an individual member of a recording group, after that group had disbanded, to perform services as a solo recording artist for the company to which he and the group were signed as exclusive recording artists? That was the issue in a decision rendered in connection with a motion for summary judgment brought in the U.S. District Court in New York.[1]

Almost four years after the Allman Brothers Band and its members entered into an exclusive recording artist agreement with Capricorn Records, Inc., they ceased to function as a group. Thereafter, Forrest Richard Betts, a singer and guitarist in the Band, notified Capricorn that because he was no longer a member of the Band, he desired to perform as a solo recording artist for a company other than Capricorn. When Capricorn refused to permit him to do so, Forrest R.B. Enterprises, Inc., the corporate employer of Betts, brought an action for a declaratory judgment to free Betts from his contractual obligations to Capricorn. Plaintiff moved for summary judgment and dismissal of certain counterclaims made by the defendant.

The sole question presented by the motion was whether, under the terms of the recording agreement, Betts was obligated individually to perform exclusive recording services for Capricorn as a solo artist, despite the dissolution of the Band as a recording group.

The opening paragraph of the agreement provided that it was made between Capricorn and five designated individuals (one of whom was Betts) "professionally known as THE ALLMAN BROTHERS BAND (hereinafter referred to as 'Artist')."

Paragraph 1 provided:

"The Artist jointly and severally hereby grants and Company engages the Artist's exclusive personal services in connection with the production of phonographic records. If this agreement is with more than one individual, this agreement shall be binding upon each

211

individual who is a signatory hereto as an Artist, jointly and severally."

Paragraph 3 of the Rider provided:

"If any member of the group shall leave the group or ceases to
perform as a member of the group, the artist and the Company may
mutually designate a new member who shall be deemed substituted
in this agreement in place of such leaving member and shall be
automatically bound by all the terms and conditions of this agreement. The artist shall execute such documents as the company may
require in connection therewith. Any such leaving member shall
continue to be bound individually by the applicable provisions of
this agreement, and shall continue to record for the Company under
each and all terms and conditions contained in his agreement except
that any such leaving artist shall receive A.F. of M. scale as his sole
advance or payment for recording hereunder and shall receive a
basic royalty of ___%."

The applicable royalty percentage was not inserted by the parties
in this paragraph.

Paragraph 14 indicated that the agreement was not to be modified
except in writing signed by both parties and was subject to the laws
of the State of Georgia.

Plaintiff, who wished to be relieved of obligations under the agreement, claimed that Rider paragraph 3 was the sole governing provision, and because the space for the applicable royalty rate was
never filled in nor made the subject of any subsequent written
agreement, said provision was unenforceable for lack of a material
term.

Defendant argued that said paragraph was inapplicable because
the Band no longer existed as a performing entity, and relied instead
on the "joint and several" language of paragraph 1, contending that
Betts' exclusive obligation as a solo performer survived the existence
of the Band. Defendant further argued alternatively that if Rider
paragraph 3 were found to control, then a triable issue of fact was
presented as to the parties' intention regarding the applicable royalty
rate.

The Court determined that Rider paragraph 3 was not controlling.
The opinion stated:

"Although the provision addresses both a 'leaving member' and
one who 'cease[s] to perform as a member of a group,' it further

recites that 'the artist and the company may mutually designate a new member who shall be deemed substituted in place of such leaving member . . .' In so providing, it indicates a primary concern with protecting the integrity of the Band as a performing entity; that is by allowing for the replacement of a member, the continued existence of the Band is contemplated. In the absence of an existing group, however, applicability of this clause would mean permitting the creation of an entirely new group, totally unrelated to the original Band. Such a situation could not possibly have been intended as encompassed within the four corners of this agreement."

The decision then stated that the ultimate question was whether the "joint and several" language of paragraph 1 merely described the nature of Betts' liability in case of breach, as plaintiff urged, or represented a separate recording obligation on the part of Betts as a solo artist despite the Band's non-existence, as defendant urged.

The motion for summary judgment was denied, but the reasoning and language of the Court in doing so is noteworthy.

The opinion notes that there is no indication within paragraph 1 or otherwise in the agreement as to whether the parties intended their joint and several obligations to survive the life of the Band. It further states:

"Although it is doubtful that the agreement would have been intended to create six separate recording contracts—with the Band and each member thereof—not only during the life of the group but also thereafter, the intention revealed by the language of paragraph 1 is sufficiently ambiguous to require some further showing."

This reasoning, and the Court's apparent willingness to allow parol evidence on the subject of the parties' intention may cause attorneys representing record companies and artists to re-evaluate contractual provisions relating to the joint and several liability of recording group members. Merely revising such provisions to specify that a member will continue to be bound under the agreement after the group has disbanded may not adequately protect the company if the agreement provides that a minimum number of recordings will be produced by the group during each specified period thereof; for in such event, each member of the group may argue that after the group has disbanded such a minimum recording commitment applies to him individually. One solution is a contractual provision which specifies that following the time when the company is notified that a group has disbanded, the company will have an option to require any of the individual members to continue to be bound as a solo artist under the terms of the agreement, with specific provisions relating to such a continuing relationship. This solution, however, requires that the company and each member of the group negotiate each of these specific provisions prior to signing an agreement. In addition to prolonging contractual negotiations, this procedure may create dissension among the members of the group if they are to receive differing advances and royalties following the dissolution of the group. Further, the company must provide that the existence of such specific provisions does not in any way constitute authorization by the company for the group to disband nor limit the remedies which the company has in the event that the group does disband.

Similarly, management companies representing groups will be well-advised to review their management contracts in light of the language of this decision.

The instant case will yield no further law on the subject, because it was settled before trial.

FOOTNOTES

1. Forrest R.B. Enterprises, Inc. v. Capricorn Records, Inc., 430 F. Supp. 849 (S.D.N.Y. 1977).

The Potent Preliminary Injunction

A preliminary injunction is a powerful remedy, often tantamount to a knock-out blow in a lawsuit. Because it is a remedy frequently sought in litigation involving the services of performers, it is a subject of which entertainers and their advisors should be aware.

A case which illustrated both the effectiveness of a preliminary injunction and the grounds on which one will be granted involved Bruce Springsteen. As a result of the injunction issued in that suit, a period of almost three years elapsed between the release of his albums, "Born To Run," and "Darkness On The Edge of Town."

Signed to an exclusive recording artist agreement with Laurel Canyon Productions, Springsteen later assented to an agreement between Laurel and CBS Records providing for Laurel to furnish Springsteen's recordings to CBS for distribution by that company.

The agreement between Laurel and CBS specified that Laurel was to designate, subject to the approval of CBS, the producers of Springsteen's albums. After the release and commercial success of "Born To Run," Springsteen advised Laurel, with the apparent acquiescence of CBS, that he intended to use Jon Landau to produce his next album, notwithstanding the objection of Laurel to this choice. (Landau had been a co-producer of the "Born To Run" album).

Laurel then made a motion for a preliminary injunction seeking to restrain Springsteen and CBS from recording albums without complying with the provisions of the operative agreements and to enjoin Springsteen from using Landau as his producer. The injunction was granted.

The reason for seeking a preliminary injunction is to preserve the status quo until the merits of the case can be heard at a later trial. This is ordinarily accomplished by the court's issuance of an order prohibiting a party from committing or continuing some action.

A court may not force an entertainer to perform services which he does not wish to render (although the performer may be held

215

liable for monetary damages caused by his refusal). In the *Springsteen* case, the court did not have the power to make him record for Laurel, only the power to prohibit him from recording for others.

Obviously, the issuance of an injunction can have significant impact on a performer's career. Accordingly, the court must be convinced of several essential elements before it will grant such relief.

First, the party claiming injury must show that money damages alone will not provide him with sufficient relief. Often this is accomplished by showing that a performer's services are unique and extraordinary and incapable of replacement. (For this reason, clauses containing such language are often found in performers' contracts). In the *Springsteen case*, the plaintiff contended that the right to name a producer was an artistic right and had more than mere commercial or monetary value.

Second, the injured party must prove that he may suffer irreparable damage if the injunction is not granted. For example, when the producer of a television series seeks to enjoin his star performer from leaving the show to perform for someone else, he will claim that the damage to his business and reputation and the loss of goodwill attendant to the association of his name with that of the departing performer all will constitute irreparable injury.

Prior to granting an injunction, the court also must be convinced that the plaintiff is likely to prevail at the ultimate trial. If the suit is based on a contract, the contractual provisions governing the relationship of the parties must be clear and unambiguous.

An injunction will not be granted if the party seeking it has "unclean hands," a phrase indicating that such party has acted in an inequitable or unfair manner.

Finally, if all of the requirements for injunctive relief are shown to exist, the court often will make a rather subjective determination: Which of the parties will be more significantly damaged if the injunction is or is not granted? Frequently, the decision of the court will turn on the answer to this question.

Variety, July 5, 1978

Compulsory Licensing of Phonorecords

The owner of copyright of a non-dramatic musical work enjoys under clauses (1) and (3) of Section 106 of the Copyright Act the exclusive rights to reproduce the work on phonorecords and distribute copies of same to the public. These exclusive rights are subject to the system of compulsory licensing for the making and distributing of phonorecords of copyrighted music set forth in Section 115 of the Act. Under this provision a musical composition that has been reproduced in phonorecords with the permission of the copyright owner generally may be so reproduced by another person if that person notifies the copyright owner and pays a specified royalty.

The first sentence of Section 115(a)(1) provides:

"When phonorecords of a nondramatic musical work have been distributed to the public in the United States under the authority of the copyright owner, any other person may, by complying with the provisions of this section, obtain a compulsory license to make and distribute phonorecords of the work."

Whereas the prior copyright law appeared to base compulsory licensing on the making or licensing of the first recording, whether or not records were distributed to the public, the new Act bases compulsory licensing on authorized public distribution of phonorecords. Sound recordings accompanying a motion picture or other audiovisiual work are not covered by these compulsory licensing provisons because such sound recordings are excluded from the definition of phonorecords.

The second sentence of clause (1) provides that: "A person may obtain a compulsory license only if his or her primary purpose in making phonorecords is to distribute them to the public for private use." This provision was the subject of substantial debate for the reasons indicated in the following quote from the House Committee Report[1] (hereafter referred to as the "House Report"):

"This provision was criticized as being discriminatory against background music systems, since it would prevent a background music producer from making recordings without the express consent of the copyright owner; it was argued that this could put the producer at a great competitive disadvantage with performing rights societies, allow discrimination, and destroy or prevent entry of businesses. The committee concluded, however, that the purpose of the compulsory license does not extend to manufacturers of phonorecords that are intended primarily for commercial use, including not only broadcasters and jukebox operators but also background music services."

The third sentence of clause (1) is intended to make clear that a person is not entitled to a compulsory license of copyrighted musical works for the purpose of making an unauthorized duplication of a musical sound recording originally developed and produced by another. The House Report states in connection with this sentence:

"Under this provision, it would be possible to obtain a compulsory license for the use of copyrighted music under Section 115 if the owner of the sound recording being duplicated authorizes its duplication. This does not, however, in any way require the owner of the original sound recording to grant a license to duplicate the original sound recording. It is not intended that copyright protection for sound recordings be circumscribed by requiring the owners of sound recordings to grant a compulsory license to unauthorized duplicators or others."

Section 115(a)(2) provides that a compulsory license allows the licensee to make a musical arrangement of the work to the extent necessary to conform it to the style or manner of interpretation of the performance involved so long as this arrangement does not change the basic melody or fundamental character of the work. Further, any such arrangement may not be claimed as a derivative work by the licensee unless the copyright owner expressly consents.

Section 115(b) deals with the notice of intention to obtain compulsory license and provides that same be served on the copyright owner (or if the registration or other public records of Copyright Office do not identify the owner, then same may be filed in the Copyright Office) before or within 30 days after making, and before distributing phonorecords of the work. Failure to serve or file the requisite notice forecloses the possibility of a compulsory license and in the absence of a negotiated license, renders the making and distribution of phonorecords actionable as acts of infringement.

Section 115(c) of the Copyright Act deals with the royalty payable under compulsory license. Clause (1) thereof states that to be entitled to receive royalties under a compulsory license "the copyright owner must be identified in the registration or other public records of the Copyright Office. The owner is entitled to royalties for phonorecords made and distributed after being so identified, but is not entitled to recover for any phonorecords previously made and distributed." This clause represents a change from the provisions of the prior law under which a copyright owner was required to file a Notice of Use in the Copyright Office in order to recover against an unauthorized manufacturer of records and reduces the possibility of a loss of rights because of failure to meet formal requirements.

Clause (2) of Section 115(c) is of substantial importance. It first provides:

"Except as provided by clause (1), the royalty under a compulsory license shall be payable for every phonorecord made and distributed in accordance with the license. For this purpose, a phonorecord is considered 'distributed' if the person exercising the compulsory license has voluntarily and permanently parted with its possession."

As stated in the House Report:

"Under the (prior) statute the specified royalty is payable 'on each such part manufactured,' regardless of how many 'parts' (i.e., records) are sold . . . (The new) basis is more compatible with the general practice in negotiated licenses today. It is unjustified to require a compulsory licensee to pay license fees on records which merely go into inventory, which may later be destroyed, and from which the record producer gains no economic benefit."

The decision contained in the House Report regarding when a licensee has "voluntarily and permanently parted with its possession" is informative. The relevant portion states:

"Under existing practices in the record industry, phonorecords are distributed to wholesalers and retailers with the privilege of returning unsold copies for credit or exchange. As a result, the number of recordings that have been 'permanently' distributed will not usually be known until some time—six or seven months on the average—after the initial distribution. In recognition of this problem, it has become a well-established industry practice, under negotiated licenses, for record companies to maintain reasonable reserves of the mechanical royalties due the copyright owners, against which royalties on the returns can be offset. The Committee recognizes that this practice may be consistent with the statutory requirements for monthly compulsory license accounting reports, but recognizes the possibility that, without proper safeguards, the maintenance of such reserves could be manipulated to avoid the making payments of the full amounts owing to copyright owners. Under these circumstances, the regulations prescribed by the Register of Copyrights should contain detailed provisions ensuring that the ultimate disposition of every phonorecord made under a compulsory license is accounted for, and that payment is made for every phonorecord 'voluntarily and permanently' distributed. In particular, the Register should prescribe a point in time when, for accounting purposes under Section 115, a phonorecord will be considered 'permanently distributed,' and should prescribe the situations in which a compulsory licensee is barred from maintaining reserves (e.g., situations in which the compulsory licensee has frequently failed to make payments in the past)."

Evidently, the Copyright Office found difficulty in establishing a uniform date on which permanent distribution is deemed to have occurred; for the supplementary information accompanying the Regulations issued by the Copyright Office to implement Section 115 of the Copyright Act[2] contains the following material:

". . . we are not persuaded on the current record that any fair basis in fact exists for the regulatory determination of a single, uniform, reserve policy for copyright purposes. The numerous factors and variables which enter into the issue of reserves (for example, configuration of phonorecord, time of year, type of music, popularity of recording artist, and sales history of producer) appear to be such as to make our determination of such a policy realistically impractical, if not impossible."

Under these circumstances, the Regulations provide in general that permanent distribution of phonorecords occurs one year from the date on which the compulsory licensee actually parts with possession, or at the time when a sale of the phonorecord is 'recognized' in accordance with generally accepted accounting principles or Internal Revenue Service practices, whichever of these events is earliest. The intent of this provision is to make the compulsory licensee's reporting requirements for copyright purposes consistent with its overall business reporting practices and requirements, an intent which is reinforced by the necessity of Certified Public Accountant certification of the annual statement of account. Section 201.19(a)(4) provides that permanent distribution occurs at the point when a phonorecord is first relinquished from possession with respect to compulsory licensees who have suffered final judgment or similar definitive finding of failure to pay mechanical royalties during a specified period.

The last sentence of Clause (2) specifies the rate of royalty with respect to each work embodied in the phonorecord and provides that same is subject to periodic reveiw by the Copyright Royalty Commission.

Clause (3) specifies that royalty payments are to be made monthly and Regulation Section 201.19 elaborates upon the monthly and annual statements of account relating to same. Clause (4) deals with the sanctions against a compulsory licensee who does not render payments and statements when due.

FOOTNOTES

1.   Report of the House Committee on the Judiciary (House Report No. 94-1476 as corrected at p. H 10727 of the *Congressional Record* for September 21, 1976).

2.   37 CFR 201.19.

Debate Over the Mechanical Royalty

After a year-long proceeding involving heated debates between copyright owners and copyright users, the Copyright Royalty Tribunal has adopted a rule adjusting the royalty rates payable under the compulsory license section of The Copyright Act of 1976.[1]

Congress characterized as "unfair" and unnecessarily burdensome on copyright owners"[2] the mechanical royalty rate of the greater of 2¾ cents for each work embodied in the phonorecord or ½ cent per minute of playing time or fraction thereof, which existed when it enacted the Copyright Revision Act of 1976:

The rule governing royalty rates adopted by the Copyright Royalty Tribunal after 46 days of hearings, with testimony from 35 witnesses representing music publishers, songwriters and record companies, among others, and over 6,000 pages of transcript, is an attempt to achieve a reasonable compromise between the demands of copyright users and copyright owners. That rule provides for an adjustment in the mechnical royalty rate "to either 4 cents, or ¾ cent per minute of playing time or fraction thereof, whichever amount is larger, for every phonorecord made and distributed on or after July 1, 1981."[3] The Tribunal determined further that, ". . . in order to insure copyright owners a continuous fair return, the above rate must be adjusted annually."[4] The adjustment would occur only if the record industry increases, during any 12 month period, the average retail list price of phonorecords.

The determination of the Copyright Royalty Tribunal was based upon the four criteria set forth in the Copyright Act of 1976:

"(A) To maximize the availability of creative works to the public;

(B) To afford the copyright owner a fair return for his creative work and the copyright user a fair income under existing economic conditions;

(C) To reflect the relative roles of the copyright owner and the copyright user in the product made available to the public with respect to relative creative contribution, technological contribution, capital investment, cost, risk, and contribution to the opening of new markets for creative expression and media for their communication;

(D) To minimize any disruptive impact on the structure of the industries involved and on generally prevailing industry practices."[5]

Throughout the Tribunal's proceedings, the copyright owners, comprising music publishers and songwriters, and represented by the National Music Publishers Association, Inc. (NMPA), the Church Music Publishers Association, the Association of Independent Music Publishers and the American Guild of Authors and Composers (AGAC), contended that the mechanical royalty be raised to 6 percent of the suggested list price, or, alternatively, that the flat rate be raised to 5 cents and adjusted annually for inflation by the Consumer Price Index.

The music publishers underlined, through studies submitted to the Tribunal, the hardship and financial risk associated with being a songwriter, and the fact that, other than performance royalties, mechanical royalties provide the major share of songwriters' income.[6] Although profits of the record industry have risen substantially, the publishers argued, the value of the mechanical royalty has been eroded; according to the Rinfret Study submitted by the publishers, the 2 cent statutory rate under the 1909 Copyright Act was the equivalent, in real purchasing terms, to 1.45 cents in 1978.[7]

The songwriters concurred with the music publishers, and indicated that inflation and the decrease in the number of songs contained on a record album had contributed to an erosion in the mechanical royalty rate not compensated for by an increase in sales volumes. Additionally, the songwriters emphasized the elimination of bargaining between copyright owners and users due to the low level of the royalty rate, and argued that a royalty rate should be set at the high end of the negotiating range to encourage bargaining and thus insure the copyright owner of a fair return[8] pursuant to the statutory criterion.

The copyright users, represented by the Recording Industry Association of America (RIAA), strenuously denied the need for any increase in the mechanical royalty rate, arguing that any such increase would be in contravention of the statutory criteria. The recording industry stressed the structural changes which have occurred in the music business, including the fact that recording costs have skyrocketed in recent years, and that record companies have taken over the tasks, formerly within the ambit of the music publishers' functions, of finding talent and developing artists' careers. Thus, the record industry argued, under the third statutory criterion requiring a comparison of the relative contributions of copyright owners and users, the findings demonstrate that the contribution of the record industry is greater.

The record industry claimed further that an increase in the mechanical royalty rate would result in staggering costs to the industry, a reduction in the number of records released, and a price rise as high as 83 cents per album which would be passed on to the consumer. The industry proposed a series of subsequent adjustments to the royalty, to occur in 1982 and 1985, proportional to the change in the average suggested list price of leading albums since 1980,[9] and therefore assertedly reflective not of external conditions, but rather of internal conditions of the industry.

The Copyright Royalty Tribunal indicated that its final ruling satisfied the statutory criteria.

First, the Tribunal found that the rate increase would "maximize the availability of creative works to the public," by providing an "economic incentive and the prospect of pecuniary rewards" to encourage the creation and dissemination of musical compositions.

Second, the Tribunal found the new rate would afford a fair return to the copyright owner and fair income to the copyright user, and would not impede the industry's growth as maintained by the copyright users.

Third, the Tribunal determined that the new mechanical royalty properly reflects the relative roles of copyright owners and users in the product made available to the public. The creative contributions on records which may be subject to the compulsory license "are made sometimes by the songwriter and music publisher, and sometimes by the record company, the copyright user."[10] Although record companies incur substantial risks and advance significant amounts of money in recording costs, the Tribunal noted the increasing ability of record companies to transfer the risk and cost of record production by means including the recoupment of costs prior to the payment of royalties, and cross-collateralization of recording artist royalties between different records.[11]

Finally, the Tribunal found that the upward adjustment of the royalty rate would not have a disruptive effect on industry structure or practices. The recording industry had successfully absorbed other cost increases without any disruptive impact, and without substantially decreasing the record company profit margin. In addition, the Tribunal found no evidence showing a direct correlation between increases in mechanical royalty rates and record company price increases passed on to the public.[12] In light of the increase between 1973 and 1979 in sales of recorded music, from $2 billion to nearly $4 billion,[13] the Tribunal determined that the new rate would provide the fairest means of assistance to the copyright owners, "subject to a price-fixed mechanical royalty in a period of great inflation."

FOOTNOTES

1.   17 U.S.C. Section 115 (1976).
2.   H.R. Rep. No. 94-1476, 94th Cong., 2d Sess. 107 (1976).
3.   *CCH Copyright Law Reports* (1981) Paragraph 13042 at CCH Ed. p. 7564.
4.   The further adjustment is as follows: For every phonorecord made and distributed on or after January 1, 1983, the royalty payable with respect to each work embodied in the phonorecord shall be either 4.25 cents, or .8 cent per minute of playing time or fraction thereof, whichever amount is larger. For every phonorecord made and distributed on or after July 1, 1984, the royalty payable with respect to each work embodied in the phonorecord shall be either 4.5 cents, or .85 cent per minute of playing time or fraction thereof, whichever amount is larger. For every phonorecord made and distributed on or after January 1, 1986, the royalty payable with respect to each work embodied in the phonorecord shall be either 5 cents, or .95 cent per minute of playing time or fraction thereof, whichever amount is larger.
5.   17 U.S.C. Section 801 (a)(1)(A) - (D) (1976).
6.   *CCH Copyright Law Reports* (1981) Paragraph 13042 at CCH Ed. p. 7533.
7.   Rinfret Study, Vol. 1, p. 24, cited in *CCH Copyright Law Reports* (1981) Paragraph 13042 at CCH Ed. p. 7531.

8. *CCH Copyright Law Reports* (1981) Paragraph 13042 at CCH Ed. p. 7537.

9. *Id.* at 7544.

10. *Id.* at 7555.

11. *Id.* at 7555.

12. *Id.* at 7563.

13. *Id.* at 7560.

Public Performance of Musical Compositions

Income derived from the public performance of musical compositions is a significant source of revenue for contemporary songwriters. Recognizing this, Congress, in the new Copyright Act ("the Act"), both expanded the protection afforded to owners for public performances of their compositions and eliminated the artificial distinction between musical works and dramatic works.

Among the rights granted to the copyright proprietor of a musical composition under the old law ("the 1909 Act") was the right to perform the work publicly for profit. If the performance was not "for profit," there was no infringement. There was no corresponding "for profit" limitation contained in the 1909 Act respecting the performance of dramatic works. Accordingly, a nonprofit institution, wishing to present the play of an author was required to obtain his permission to do so but that same organization wishing to perform a musical composition of that author did not require his permission.

The Act eliminates this distinction. Section 106 grants the copyright proprietor the exclusive rights "in the case of literary, musical, dramatic and choreographic works, pantomimes and motion pictures and other audiovisual works, to perform the copyrighted work publicly."

This provision no longer contains the "for profit" limitation of the 1909 Act. The House Committee Report relating to this elimination states:

"The line between commercial and 'non-profit' organizations is increasingly difficult to draw. Many 'non-profit-organizations are highly subsidized and capable of paying royalties, and the widespread public exploitation of copyrighted works by public broadcasters and other non-commercial organizations is likely to grow. In addition to these trends, it is worth noting that performances and displays are continuing to supplant markets for printed copies and that in the future a broad 'not for profit' exemption could not only hurt authors, but could dry up their incentive to write."[1]

Section 110 of the Act specifies ten categories which, notwithstanding the exclusive rights granted performances in Section 106, do not constitute an infringement of copyright. Generally, they include a) performance in the course of face-to-face teaching activities of a nonprofit educational institute; b) instructional broadcasting; c) performance during the course of a religious service; d) performance other than by transmission to the public which have no direct or indirect commercial advantage for which neither performer, promoters or organizers are paid and for which no admission is charged, or if charged, used for private financial gain; e) communication of a transmission of a performance on an ordinary radio or television provided that no admission is charged and that the transmission is not further transmitted to the public; f) performance by a vending establishment open to the public at large where the sole purpose of the performance is to promote the retail sales of copies or phonorecords of the work.

The 1909 Act contained no definition of what constituted a "public" performance. As a result courts decided the issue on a case by case basis. Section 101 of the Act remedies this by defining "publicly" to include any performance at any place open to the public or at any place where a substantial number of persons outside of a normal circle of a family and its social acquaintances is gathered.

The legislation also provides that "public" includes "semi-public" places. Regarding this provision, the House Report states: "One of the principal purposes of the definition was to make clear that . . . performances in 'semi-public' places, such as clubs, lodges, factories, summer camps and schools, are 'public performances' subject to copyright control."[2]

Further, one article[3] on the subject has reached the following conclusions regarding the liability of an owner of a "public" place in which copyrighted music is played:

a) If the musicians are independent contractors over whom the proprietor of the place of business has no control, that proprietor is nevertheless liable for the musicians' performance of copyrighted music;

b) If the proprietor instructs the musicians not to play certain music, he is liable if the musicians nevertheless play the music;

c) If the proprietor does not pay the musicians but merely allows them to come in, play and collect tips, he is nevertheless liable for unauthorized performances.

FOOTNOTES

1. H.R. No. 1476, 94th Cong., 2d Sess. 62-63 (1976).

2. *Id.* at 64.

3. Goldstein, "Questions and Answers About the Performance of Music Under the New Copyright Law," *California State Bar Journal,* July/August 1978, Vol. 53 No. 4, p.238.

Chapter Eight
New Technologies

Videocassettes and Videodiscs

The home video market has become a meaningful source of ancillary income for producers and distributors of entertainment productions and in some instances represents a possible market for the production of original programming.

The video cassette recorder ("VCR") was the first device which gave the home viewer a chance to watch television programming and theatrical movies when and where he wanted. Consumer acceptance has been widespread, sales having increased each year since Sony introduced its Betamax VCR in 1975.

The VCR enables the viewer to play back through his system both pre-recorded material such as motion pictures and programs which he has recorded from his television set or other sources.

There are two VCR formats: the Beta format developed by Sony and the video home system format ("VHS") developed by Matsushita. They are incompatible in that Beta format tapes cannot be played on the VHS system and vice versa.

The Sony Betamax is the best known of the Beta systems, but Sony licenses its system to other companies such as Zenith, Toshiba, Sanyo and Sears. The VHS system, which has significantly more sales than the Beta system, is licensed to companies such as RCA, General Electric, Hitachi, Magnavox, Panasonic and Sylvania.

At present, Japan is the largest manufacturer and purchaser of VCRs. The United States represents a strong market for these machines as do other countries of the world, particularly England and Europe, in which a wide variety of television programs is not available.

The video disc player, unlike the VCR, primarily is a playback only system. The discs now being manufactured have no capacity to record (although companies are developing erasable discs that are recorded with a laser and can be reused like videotape). Significant amounts of money have been invested in the development of

235

this technology, RCA alone having spent between $150 million and $200 million in the creation of its SelectaVision system.

The logic behind the development of the video disc player is that "VCR's are primarily a product for people wanting to 'time shift' television programs broadcast when they're not at home or otherwise occupied, or to produce video 'home movies' and that there is a separate market composed of people who just want the playback capability videodiscs offer at lower costs for both machines and program material."[1] To this must be added the potential offered by interactivity, or viewer participation, as noted below.

There are three competing videodisc systems which, like the two VCR systems, are incompatible.

SelectaVision uses a system similar to audio records in which a stylus is guided by grooves in the disc surface to decode information recorded as pits in the electrically conductive material of the disc. Because these pits vary the capacitance[2] of the surface points, this disc is referred to as a capacitance electronic disc. Mechanical contact is made between the stylus and the disc; thus for protection, the disc is packaged in a sleeve which is removed only after insertion into the player.

Although the RCA system does have the ability to locate the beginning of a particular program segment quite rapidly, the player initially released by it lacked the random access capability of its competitor systems. (In September 1983, RCA introduced an interactive random access player which can be programmed to find any segment on a disc instantly.)

MCA, Inc. and N.V. Philips developed the laser vision optical disc technique. This system uses a laser to scan a disc on which a video signal in the form of a reflective coding has been recorded. This disc supposedly is unaffected by dirt and scratches.

Because a laser scans the grooves of the disc and does not touch its surface, it can be sent from one segment or frame to another in any order that the viewer wishes, and virtually instantaneously. The result is that the material contained on the disc need not be presented in a linear format, but rather may be produced so that the viewer can interact with or participate in the program that is being played.

The third disc system is known as the video high density ("VHD") system. A series of release dates in the United States have been postponed and presently the system is commercially available only in Japan. Although it is "a capacitance system using a contact stylus like RCA's, VHD has two important differences that make it incompatible with RCA technology but at the same time permit a broader range of features. The discs do not have a groove to guide the stylus along the pitted recording tracks, instead using separate 'tracking pits' laid between the main tracks to carry information used to position and guide the stylus . . . Because it isn't locked into following a groove, the stylus is free to be directed laterally across the surface of the disc while the disc spins . . . With that freedom, (the developer of the system) claims, VHD will permit random access, still frames, and a variety of slow and fast speeds in forward and reverse."[3]

There are several interesting issues which have resulted from the growth of the home video market. One, of course, is the use of VCRs to tape programs which are presented on television, a subject which is the core of much publicized litigation and proposed legislation.

Another is raised by the marketing policies of distributors of videocassettes. Because of the first sale doctrine embodied in the copyright laws, when a videocassette is sold the copyright proprietor no longer controls the product nor shares in income derived by the purchaser/retailer who may then elect to rent the videocassette to the consumer. An executive of a major distributor has stated: "We can't stand by and watch an ever-expanding universe in which rental revenues which we do not participate in get larger and larger and continue to invest millions of dollars in the films to fuel this market and not get any of it back."[4]

To counter this problem, some videocassette distributors tried, with little success thus far, to initiate a rental-only policy. Others have lowered the retail list price to $29.95 and $39.95 from prices as high as $69.95. This approach has resulted in higher sales and possibly will become more widespread. As various marketing policies are investigated there is a simultaneous lobbying effort being conducted with the goal of modifying laws relating to the first sales doctrine.

A third issue has been the devastating effect of worldwide copying of programs contained on videocassettes and the impact which this has had on the sales of the product.

Because of the significant sums of money which are now available from exploitation in the home video market, the pattern by which a motion picture is exploited (theatrical release, pay television exhibition, network television broadcast, television syndication) has been altered. Motion pictures now are released by means of videocassettes and videodiscs while the picture is being exhibited in motion picture theaters during its initial run. One report indicates that home video in Europe may replace theaters as the major medium of film viewing, and a survey conducted by a British company predicts that the home video explosion will have an effect on cinema attendance in the 1980s similar to that of television in the 1950s when British cinema audiences were reduced from 23 million people a week in 1955 to under 10 million people a week by 1960. Today the number is less than 2 million people a week.[5]

A prominent independent producer prophesied that: "In 10 years' time I believe people will be able to go to the cinema free, or at least for a nominal fee . . . Pop records are sold through radio airplay, and the cinema of the future will work the same way. People will be able to see a new film free for perhaps a week. That will build word of mouth and other people will want to buy or rent the video to watch the film at home."[6]

Agreements pertaining to programs produced in the first instance for distribution on videodiscs and videocassettes present several interest problems. Although the product which is the subject of the agreement is viewed on a television screen, that product is marketed more in the form of a record than a television program. In addition to issues relating to production are those relating to payment of royalty recipients. These are paid a percentage of net receipts of the distributor or the net wholesale price of the disc or cassette, rather than a percentage of net profits. Questions familiar to attorneys who have negotiated record agreements such as whether and to what extent the distributor is entitled to a packaging deduction, to distribute product as so-called free goods, to withhold reserves against returns of product, to distribute product by means of clubs and other similar plans must be addressed. Also, a participant must negotiate the manner in which he is to participate in rental or leasing receipts, especially when his royalties are computed on the basis of the wholesale selling price of the videocassette rather than on the basis of net receipts derived by the distributor.

Further, various unions are keenly aware of the impact of home video and continue to address this market in their negotiations. Accordingly, each union agreement must be examined by producers who produce for the home video market.

Finally, items which are required to be delivered in connection with the production of programs for motion picture and television purposes may differ from delivery items required in the production of interactive videodiscs; for these discs utilize computer techniques and delivery items may include materials described in computer terminology.

FOOTNOTES

1. *Broadcast,* February 2, 1981, p.35.

2. "Capacitance" is defined in Webster's New Collegiate Dictionary as "the property of an electric non-conductor that permits the storage of energy as a result of electric displacement when opposite surfaces of the non-conductor are maintained at a difference of potential."

3. *Id.* at p.38.

4. Variety, November 11, 1981, p.1, quoting Leon Knize, Marketing Senior Vice President of Warner Home Video.

5. *Hollywood Reporter,* October 6, 1981.

6. *Id.* at p. S-3, quoting David Puttnam.

High Definition Television

The technology of high definition television ("HDTV") dramatically increases the quality of visual images which appear on a television screen. Several producers, executives and craftspeople who have worked with or analyzed this technology compare the difference between the present television picture and that offered by HDTV to the difference between black and white and color television.

"The moving television picture is actually a series of still pictures displayed sequentially at a rate rapid enough to give the impression of continuous motion. Each frame is created by scanning a beam of electrons in a horizontal line from left to right and from top to bottom over the face of a phosphor-coated tube. The number of any scanning lines in any system determines the accuracy or resolution of the reproduced picture."[1]

In the United States and Japan, the NTSC color television standard is used. This standard contains 525 horizontally scanned lines which are displayed at a rate of 30 frames per second. In Europe and other areas, the PAL or SECAM standards contain 625 lines. The NTSC standard also utilizes a broadcast width to height ratio of 4:3.

The technology of HDTV displayed to the public in the United States by CBS was created primarily by the Japanese Broadcasting Corporation, Panasonic, Sony and Ikegami, and utilizes 1,125 scanning lines as opposed to 525 or 625 lines. The system also employs a broader width to height ratio—5:3 as opposed to 4:3—and features enhanced color reproduction and fidelity as well as a stereophonic audio capacity. As a result, approximately five times the standard amount of picture information is presented on each frame, causing significantly enhanced image quality, colors and sharpness of picture.

Proponents of HDTV are hopeful that it will herald the advent of "electronic cinematography" as an alternative to the present television practice of shooting many programs (with situation comedies a notable exception) on 35mm film and then transferring them to tape. The present practice endures because of the disparity between the contrast ratio of film and videotape; HDTV lessens this disparity.

Francis Ford Coppola, an innovative theatrical producer and ardent supporter of HDTV, testifying before the House Communications Subcommittee, stated:

"Television is an electronic medium and this creates images and sounds solely through the manipulation of electricity. The fact that it has no substance other than energy makes it ideally suited for manipulation, processing, handling and combining with other immages and matting . . . Film on the other hand is a physical substance, its images and sound recorded through chemistry. Therefore, it can only be edited or manipulated by cutting with a razor and literally Scotch-taping together in new combinations. It is extremely difficult to combine or matte with other images, and in general is slow and costly to creatively handle and transport. However, photographic film is a medium at the apogee of its development; it is able to record the picture in unmatchable color, clarity and luster. Television, by comparison, is a poor second place when it comes to image quality. Obviously, something is desired that has the flexibility and speed of handling and distribution to the public of television and yet matches the image quality of photographic film. High-definition television promises to be the first phase of such an ideal new medium."[2]

If successful, HDTV will have applications which extend to Direct Broadcast Satellites ("DBS"), motion pictures, videocassettes, videodiscs, cable television, videotex, teletext, and teleconferencing.

CBS' application to the FCC contemplates a three channel HDTV DBS service. Its proposal indicates that the first channel would supply advertiser-supported programming to local affiliates for terrestrial retransmission and to those homes equipped with roof-top dishes located outside the service area of CBS affiliates. The second channel would distribute pay programming, such as entertainment, cultural, sports, news and religious programs, to cable systems and direct to homes. The third channel would offer other subscriber services, satellite to theater distribution and closed circuit transmissions.

Other DBS applicants also have mentioned HDTV service, although not to the same degree as has CBS.

In regard to motion pictures, if HDTV technology were to become competitive in quality with film, then advocates of HDTV contend that for each successful picture millions of dollars in production and delivery costs could be saved. Currently, between 1,000 and 1,500 prints of a film, costing from $800 to $1,600 each, are made for distribution purposes. Transmitting HDTV to theaters by satellite, cable or otherwise could save a substantial portion of these costs and the costs of delivery and print replacement. However, HDTV projectors cost approximately four times more than conventional 35mm projection equipment and theaters also might need to purchase or lease satellite receiving stations to receive the HDTV signal.

A report entitled "High Definition Television to the Year 2000"[3] postulates that the first availability of HDTV will occur before mid-decade to a small number of consumers in both Japan and the U.S. by means of videocassettes and cable television. This report further anticipates that by 1990 there will be a cumulative total of approximately 500,000 HDTV videocassette and videodisc players in the United States.

Obstacles do exist which must be overcome in the development of HDTV service.

In an era of spectrum scarcity, HDTV requires a wide bandwidth, much wider than is able to fit within conventional VHF and UHF channels. In this regard, HDTV is allied with the development of digital technology which has the ability to compress the bandwidth of signals, thus achieving more spectrum efficiency.

This obstacle is not as meaningful in providing HDTV service by cable television, which does not have the same concerns regarding spectrum availability. Cable systems with numerous channels will accomodate an HDTV service taking advantage of wide bandwidths and under-used channel capacity. Accordingly, cable television appears to be comparatively well-suited to provide HDTV program service.

Also, to be effective in television production, HDTV cameras will have to be smaller and more lightweight than those used to date in experimental HDTV productions. It has been stated that the next necessary hurdle for HDTV will be "a sort of quantum leap in the size of cameras and other production equipment."[4]

Finally, the costs of an HDTV set will be higher than a conventional television set and the screen size will be bigger. In the early years of the existence of HDTV, the costs will be considerably higher than they will be as the medium develops. For this reason, HDTV may lead to an active market in the rental of HDTV sets.

Even with these obstacles, it is apparent from the reactions of those who have seen HDTV that this new technology will have a significant impact on the entertainment industry and will provide an arena in which the technical and artistic communities can work jointly to benefit the industry.

FOOTNOTES

1. *Broadcasting*, February 1, 1982 at 82.

2. *Id.* at 84, quoting the testimony of Francis Ford Coppola before the House Telecommunications Subcommittee, December, 1981.

3. M. Guite, V. Weston and C. Bowen, *High Definition Television to the Year 2000, A Report For CBS Television Network* (January 1982) by Kalba Bowen Associates, Inc.).

4. *Broadcasting, supra*, at 86, quoting Ron Colby of Zoetrope Studios.

Teletext and Videotex

Teletext and videotex may be years away from widespread public consumption in the United States, but they have been the subject of frequent news reports, analyses, tests, conferences and announcements by major companies. Several of the latter seem to have brought teletext and videotex closer to the ambit of the entertainment industry by stressing that the scope of their operations will extend to entertainment uses of these technologies.

Teletext and videotex information distribution services, often labelled "electronic publishing," are means of disseminating text and graphic information by electronic means for display on terminals which are under the selective control of the recipient. The data may be transmitted by television channels, FM radio broadcasting, microwave, phone line circuits, cable or a combination of the above.

Teletext is a one-way system whereas videotex is an interactive, or two-way, system.

A common method of transmitting data by teletext is to insert messages in the unused lines of the vertical blanking interval of the normal television broadcast signal. This interval is a black bar that appears between pictures when the signal is rolled vertically. Current teletext experiments use only two to six of the 525 lines that make up the television signal that is used in the United States. The teletext signal is detected by a special decoder that either is a separate accessory to the TV receiver or built into the receiver. When the viewer presses an indexed code on his control pad the desired "page" of information is transferred to the television screen by means of the decoder circuitry. The teletext data may be the only material on the screen, overlay part of the picture or appear in a box or window on the screen.

The following is a manner in which a recipient might utilize teletext: "A demonstration videotape of the (teletext) services described people planning a night out in San Diego by picking the

245

type of food they want and the area they want to eat in. The set then displays a list of restaurants of the right kind in the right location and provides the menu of each. Another query gives them a list of movie theaters in that neighborhood and what is playing in each. On the other hand, a person who stays at home could query the television set for a recipe for veal that would cost under $9 for four servings . . . The system does not require two-way capability, but it does require a decoder to pluck the desired data from the store of information (that will be kept) on tap and updated at intervals that will vary according to whether it is the odds on the upcoming fight or the population of Omaha."[1]

Videotex is a two-way system in which the viewer can request information from a computer data base containing enormous amounts of information (75,000 to 100,000 "pages" of information as opposed to approximately 200 "pages" now being used in over-the-air teletext tests). Typically, the phone line will link the user to the information source, although other methods such as cable television and microwave techniques can be employed. The customer can receive such information as up-to-the-minute stock quotation, airline or train schedules and local houses for sale on the screen of the home or office television set.

In a recent speech, an advocate of videotex technology described the following scenario:

"Beyond the normal menu of news, weather, sports, even astrology, subscribers would learn—through advertisements—of items for sale in local stores. Then, using the same terminal, they would place an order with the stores. Once they have bought, say, film from a local photo shop, 'they'll be able to check out how much money they've got in their checking account. And if they want to, automatically pay some bills. So what we're talking about is another step towards a cashless society . . . or at least a less cash society.' "[2]

As in the videocassette and videodisc industries, there are competing technological systems and little standardization. In Britain, two television organizations, the British Broadcasting Corporation and Independent Television have been transmitting broadcast teletext for years. The BBC's tradename for its teletext system is Ceefax. In 1977, the British Post Office launched its system of videotex called Prestel. In France and Canada, systems designated as Antiope and Telidon, respectively, have been developed.

A North American standard, based on a system developed by AT&T and known as Presentational Level Protocol Syntax ("PLPS") was accepted by two groups, the American National Standards Institute and the Canadian Standards Association, which have been negotiating to arrive at a common teletext-videotex formula for North America.

Proponents of PLPS stress the more impressive graphics and colors available with the North American Standard while advocates of the British system cite its cost effectiveness. It is possible that the Federal Communications Commission will not take any action toward setting standards for the business; in broadcast teletext, the FCC's primary concern is for efficient spectrum allocation.

Besides the lack of standardization, those investing in teletext and videotex must deal with several difficult issues. Should the service be supported by advertising (particularly teletext) or be financed by charging the recipient? Regarding videotex, is telephone or cable technology better suited to the medium? What information contained in data banks will be of greatest interest to consumers? Should a company create or acquire from others the information in the data bank?

Numerous legal issues also must be faced in connection with the transmission of data by means of teletext and videotex. In regard to videotex, issues exist regarding the protection of the data transmitted and the interception of messages. Also, because subscribers may be shopping or paying bills from their homes, an enormous amount of information regarding that subscriber will be compiled and questions arise as to whether this information may be made available to law enforcement agencies, direct mailers, credit investigators or poll takers. Further problems such as unauthorized copying and the transfer by a subscriber of material to his own data bank will abound as will questions regarding content liability, obscenity and equal access in political campaigns.

This is a period of testing to ascertain answers to the foregoing questions and also to learn whether the data capabilities of these technologies can be harnessed for entertainment uses.

For example, will the number of subscribers who are willing to pay to watch a boxing event be increased by having an announcer invite viewers to vote on the boxer that they feel won each round? Further, will viewers respond to the opportunity of being able to request a specific type of programming, such as a comedy program on Monday night between 8 and 10 PM?

Together with videocassettes, videodiscs and videogames, videotex and teletext have contributed to the dramatic change in the relationship between the viewer and his home television and have increased the options available to satisfy his informational and entertainment requirements.

FOOTNOTES

1.   Ralph Tyler, "Changing Channels, Part VI: Predictions for a Wired Future," *On Cable*, April 1982.

2.   *Broadcasting*, June 28, 1982, p.49, quoting from a speech by J. Roger Moody, Vice President, Development for CBS, Inc.

Distribution of Non-Standard Television Signals

The methods by which television signals are distributed to viewers have become meaningful not only to those who are interested in technology but also to attorneys, representatives and program suppliers who negotiate for "non-standard" rights.

The term "non-standard television" has been used by several companies involved in cable and pay television to define the areas in which the rights to programming which they are licensing will be exclusive to them. One major company recently defined "non-standard television" as: "any and all forms of television exhibition and display, whether now-existing or developed in the future, other than exhibition by means of Standard Television; 'non-standard television' includes, without limitation, cable television, 'over-the-air' subscription or pay television, pay cable television, direct-by-satellite (DBS), master antenna television, closed-circuit television, hotel, motel or hospital room service, and all cassette, disc and multipoint distribution service exhibitions (excluding Consumer Video Uses), all on a subscription, license, rental, sale, or any other basis."

"Standard television" is then defined to mean:

"non-pay, UHF or VHF broadcast television throughout the universe transmitted solely by means of one or more local broadcast stations and intended for intelligible reception in the localities of such broadcast stations by the general public by means of standard home antennas."

These definitions make reference to three forms of distribution technologies: radiating, non-radiating and storage. The latter, which refers to a technology in which a signal is allowed to pause for a period of time between its point of acquisition and its point of usage (videodiscs and videocassettes in particular) has been discussed in a previous article (see p. 235). It should be noted, however, that the reference in the definition to cassette and disc exhibitions should not be read to refer to the distribution of cassettes and discs to the public for viewing in the home. Rather, the reference pertains to the instance when a signal stored on a cassette or disc is transmitted by one of the other technologies referred to in the definition.

Radiating distribution does not require a physical connection to the source of the signal. An ordinary television transmitter which transmits broadcast signals is an example of a radiating technology. Television stations often use high powered transmissions from tall towers to enable the signal to travel long distances. An emerging form of radiating distribution is low power television (LPTV) which broadcasts original programming.

It is not uncommon for a low power transmission system to receive a television broadcast on a particular channel, to "translate" the signal from one frequency to another and then to broadcast the translated signal on a separate channel. The transmissions of these translators covers small areas.

Construction permits for LPTV stations will be granted by the FCC first for rural areas and then for inner cities. It is estimated that "when it's all over, perhaps as many as 10,000 new mini-stations will have at least a chance to make it in the broadcasting business."[1]

Some of these LPTV channels will simply rebroadcast network feeds but others will add local programming and some may scramble their signals and make viewers pay for the right to descramble them.

Multi-Point Distribution Services (MDS) normally transmit over the air by means of an extremely high frequency microwave signal from a fixed station to a receiving antenna device. The signal then is converted to a lower frequency, thus enabling it to be viewed on an unused VHF channel. Ordinarily, the range of the microwave signal does not exceed 25 miles and the signal will be affected by terrain or other obstacles in its line of sight transmission.

Multi-Point Distribution Services are common carriers and are regulated by the FCC. At present, pay television services are their prime customers. Because receivers capable of intercepting signals are relatively inexpensive to build, MDS operators, like so many others in the entertainment industry, are grappling with the problems of piracy. MDS systems, however, do offer an advantage versus cable systems in that the start-up costs and operating costs of the former are considerably less than those of the latter. The market for MDS (as for STV and DBS to be discussed below) will be in areas with low population density or which otherwise are uneconomical for wiring by cable companies.

Subscription television (STV) is a system in which a standard television signal is transmitted carrying premium programming in a scrambled form. The subscriber pays an installation fee plus a monthly charge for a decoder which descrambles the signal.

STV is received in significantly more homes than MDS and is an important consideration of any entrepreneur who intends to distribute an event to the public on a pay-per-view basis.

As with MDS, the start-up and operating costs for an STV system are significantly less than those for a cable system, and because it normally transmits on a single assigned channel, the channel capacity offered by STV is significantly more limited than that offered by cable. Although a few companies are developing multi-channel decoders for STV which may increase the number of channels which can be transmitted, this disparity vis-à-vis cable will remain.

Communications satellites have had an immense impact on the transmission of non-standard television signals, especially since 1975 when Home Box Office began to use satellites for the transmission of its programming service. These satellites were described as early as 1945 when Arthur C. Clarke wrote in "Wireless World" of a "geosynchronous satellite" which, if placed in orbit 22,300 miles above the equator would have the same rotational velocity as that of the earth, thereby appearing to remain in a fixed position above a given point on the earth.

To receive signals from a communications satellite, an earth station (down-link) is required. Because the number of television stations, cable systems, hotels, apartments and individuals have acquired earth stations, the number of services making use of communication satellites for transmission of signals has increased dramatically.

Direct Broadcast Satellites (DBS) transmit signals which are more powerful than those of communications satellites because their transmissions are intended for direct receipt by consumers who have earth stations which are significantly smaller than those required for the communications satellite. To transmit the stronger signal comparatively large transponders are required; thus, DBS may have only three or four transponders as opposed to the 24 which many communications satellites now use.

In order to receive a DBS signal, there must be a clear path between the satellite and the earth station. Studies indicate that as a result the primary recipients of DBS signals will be subscribers who live in rural, unobstructed areas.

The FCC has allocated a portion of the broadcast spectrum for DBS use and has adopted a "flexible regulatory approach." DBS operators may experiment with the type of service they offer; some may choose to be common carriers, others may offer original programming.

DBS proposals indicate that some operators intend to offer sophisticated services which may include high-definition television, stereophonic sound, teletext and/or dual-language soundtracks.

Of the forms of non-radiating distribution, telephone wires are the least useful for television transmission, coaxial cable has had the greatest impact in the area of non-standard television and fiber optics are the most sophisticated.

Ordinary telephone wires are not particularly effective for the transmission of the typical television signal. In England, however, several cable television systems transmit programs on transmission systems which are the equivalent of telephone wires.

Community antenna television systems began utilizing coaxial cable in the late 1940s in order to increase the number of television signals that viewers in remote areas were able to receive and to improve signal reception for viewers who lived in obstructed areas. These systems were the forerunners of the cable television systems of today, some of which offer in excess of 100 channels.

The cable system carries basic services (those which the subscriber receives without paying an amount in excess of his basic monthly charge) and premium services (those for which the subscriber pays such an additional monthly amount).

Premium programming transmitted by cable is not immune to piracy. Among the security mechanisms that are being attempted to prevent theft of programming is "channel trapping," a method by which the channels used for premium programming are filtered out of the feed to non-subscribers of the system.

Fiber optics are in their infancy, but offer several advantages over telephone wires and cable. These tiny, lightweight, flexible glass wires are less expensive than wire and offer the capability of accomodating channels far in excess of even the 100 channels presently being used in the most sophisticated cable systems.

The government of France will use fiber optic technology in connection with the wiring of approximately 1.4 million French homes at a cost estimated to be in excess of $1 billion. The experience of that endeavor may have a significant impact on the manner in which fiber optics are used in future situation.

It is apparent that the above definition of non-standard television is broad and encompasses several forms of distribution technology. In negotiations when this definition is an issue, the attorney should evaluate each element which is included and, if possible, exclude those which are inapplicable under the circumstances.

FOOTNOTES

1. *Broadcasting*, October 11, 1982, p. 46.

The Videogame License

The marriage of entertainment with microelectronics has spawned the highly publicized videogame business. One company is reported to have paid $21 million for videogame rights to a character and estimated (erroneously, it turns out) that its wholesale revenues from a game using that character would exceed $100 million.

The home videogames which have enjoyed the greatest success thus far have been based upon popular arcade games. However, there is significant competition among manufacturers to obtain rights to well-known characters (E.T., Spiderman, The Incredible Hulk) and titles ("Raiders of the Lost Ark," "Star Wars").

The agreements under which these characters and titles ("licensed elements") are licensed to manufacturers of videogames are similar to licensing arrangements in general, although several aspects deserve particular comment.

The licensor will grant to the videogame manufacturer the exclusive license during the basic term to utilize the licensed element in the manufacture, distribution, sale, rental and advertising of videogames for use on videogame machines.

The definition of licensed element may include any voices, movements, personalities, logos, trademarks and names associated therewith, as well as any forms in which the element may have been depicted in literary, musical, motion picture, dramatic, pictorial, graphic or sculptural works.

The licensor must review the grant language with care to make certain that the rights granted are those which it alone controls without obligation to any third party. For example, if the right to use a voice associated with the licensed element is incorporated in the grant, is there any requirement that permission be obtained from or payment made to the performer whose voice is used?

Under the above grant, the product in which the licensee may use the licensed element is a videogame, which has been defined as software for use in a hardware unit that produces an electronically generated audio-visual display for entertainment purposes and game play. That grant also indicates that the videogames be used on videogame machines.

The parties may wish to specify that the videogame be marketed solely for use in the home, thus negating the possible interpretation that licensee is granting the right to produce arcade games.

The requirement in the grant that the software be used on videogame machines is crucial, but may require further elaboration.

Large numbers of personal home computers are being sold. Those computers bearing higher prices generally have large memories and are purchased for reasons other than game playing. Manufacturers of videogame machines are concerned, however, that low-priced computers are being marketed and/or purchased primarily as devices for playing videogames.

Several issues are presented because of the foregoing: (1) Does the licensee have the right to manufacture videogames for use on computers? (2) Does the licensor retain that right, and if so, may licensor exercise that right during the basic term? (3) If the licensor may exercise that right, may it do so with respect to all computers or only the so-called high end computer, thus alleviating some of the direct competition with licensee's product which would result if videogames embodying the licensed element were sold for use on low end computers? (4) If licensee is restricted from granting rights in the licensed element for videogame use on computers, does that restriction pertain to educational methods (which may or may not be structured in game form) and computer literacy programs?

These questions are fundamental ones in defining both the grant and the reservation of rights.

There are three concepts to consider regarding the term of the agreement: (1) the basic term; (2) the distribution period for each videogame which is manufactured, and (3) the sell-off period.

During the basic term, often two or three years, the licensee has exclusive rights to the licensed element in the defined product category and the licensor may be precluded from making certan exploitations of the licensed element.

There will be no incentive for the licensee to create new videogames towards the end of the basic term if it does not have sufficient time to market those games. Therefore, the licensee may be granted a minimum period during which it can sell, distribute and exploit each game which was created and first manufactured during the basic term. Thus, it is possible that following the basic term the original licensee is exploiting new videogames using that element.

At the end of the distribution period the licensee may have on hand an inventory of product which it wishes to "sell-off" for a limited time period It is not unusual for the licensor to grant such a sell-off period conditioned on the requirement that the licensee shall not have manufactured excessive quantities of games during the months preceding the expiration of the distribution period.

In most licensing arrangements it is important that the licensor have input into and exercise control over the creation and marketing of the derivative product in order to properly protect its rights in the licensed element. When dealing in software for videogames these controls are of particular importance. First, the replication of the licensed element in the game will be quite different from the replication of that element in literary works, merchandise, movies or television because, in the former, an entirely new configuration guided by electronic impluses is created. When a company licenses the right to depict E.T. on a T-shirt, it has a much better idea of what to expect of the finished product than it does when it allows a third party to create a videogame using that character. Second, manufacturers are learning that although attaching a recognizable name to a game is helpful in attracting consumers it is at least as important that the game be one which is effective.

Accordingly, most licensors of recognizable licensed elements will demand input and controls at all stages of the development of the game, including creating of concept, storyboard, artwork, audiovisual display, testing and completion. Ordinarily, the licensor will not have approval over engineering design and electronic components.

In order to maximize its potential revenue, the licensor may request that the licensee release no less than a specified number of different videogames during each year of the basic term and expend a minimum amount of money advertising and promoting the products.

As compensation, the licensor customarily will be paid a combination of advances against royalties, guarantees and royalties.

Typically, the licensor will be paid a royalty based upon either the wholesale selling price of the game or upon licensee's net receipts.

In some instances, licensor's royalty will be computed on the basis of the suggested retail list price of the product.

In negotiations regarding the amount and computation of licensor's royalty it is helpful to have knowledge of the distribution policies of the licensee. To what extent are free goods and promotional products distributed? Are the products of that company distributed in conjunction with premium plans? What is the policy regarding returns, credits, allowances, discounts, and withholding of taxes? In each instance in which the response is a cause for concern the licensee may wish to provide for appropriate compromises.

Further, licensor may consider it appropriate to demand a different royalty computation for income derived from the rental as opposed to the sale of products, because licensee's expenses in connection with the former are far less than the latter. At times a licensor who is receiving a royalty of 7 to 10 percent of the wholesale selling price will request 25 to 50 percent of licensee's income derived from rental activities.

The license agreement also should address the issue of which party owns each of the various elements (including the copyright, when applicable) of the videogame, such as the storyline, audiovisual display, licensed element, title of the game and the source code and object code of the programming.

Once ownership is established the parties must focus on the corollary issue of whether there are any restrictions on the owner's exercise of such rights.

For example, if the licensor owns the storyline, may the licensor allow a television program utilizing that storyline to be broadcast during the basic term? May either party produce a movie having the same title as that of the videogame? May the licensor market an article of merchandise during the basic term using a name of description which is the same as the title of a videogame produced under the agreement?

As in all licensing arrangements the representations, warranties and indemnities of each party must be negotiated at length and specified in detail in the agreement.

The videogame industry is in the early stages of its growth, yet complex questions already have arisen to tax the skills of those who negotiate and prepare the license agreements which are involved.

Table of Cases

Table of Cases

Index

Index